<u>Disclaimer</u>

Book Title: An Ontology of Identity Credentials Part 1: Background and Formulation

Book Author: An Ontology of Identity Credentials Part 1: Background and Formulation

Book Abstract: The Information Technology Laboratory (ITL) at the National Institute of Standards and Technology (NIST) promotes the U.S. economy and public welfare by providing technical leadership for the Nation s measurement and standards infrastructure. ITL develops tests, test methods, reference data, proof of concept implementations, and technical analyses to advance the development and productive use of information technology. ITL s responsibilities include the development of management, administrative, technical, and physical standards and guidelines for the cost-effective security and privacy of non-national security-related information in Federal information systems. This special publication 800-series reports on ITL s research, guidelines, and outreach efforts in information system security, and its collaborative activities with industry, government, and academic organizations.

Citation: NIST SP - 800-103

NIST Special Publication 800-103
Draft

An Ontology of Identity Credentials
Part 1: Background and Formulation

**National Institute of
Standards and Technology**
Technology Administration
U.S. Department of Commerce

**William MacGregor
William Dutcher
JamilKhan**

INFORMATION SECURITY

Information Technology Laboratory
National Institute of Standards and Technology
Gaithersburg, MD, 20899-8930

October 2006

U.S. Department of Commerce
Carlos M. Gutierrez, Secretary

Technology Administration
Robert C. Cresanti, Under Secretary of Commerce for
Technology

National Institute of Standards and Technology
William Jeffrey, Director

Reports on Computer Systems Technology

The Information Technology Laboratory (ITL) at the National Institute of Standards and Technology (NIST) promotes the U.S. economy and public welfare by providing technical leadership for the Nation's measurement and standards infrastructure. ITL develops tests, test methods, reference data, proof of concept implementations, and technical analyses to advance the development and productive use of information technology. ITL's responsibilities include the development of management, administrative, technical, and physical standards and guidelines for the cost-effective security and privacy of non-national security-related information in Federal information systems. This special publication 800-series reports on ITL's research, guidelines, and outreach efforts in information system security, and its collaborative activities with industry, government, and academic organizations.

National Institute of Standards and Technology Special Publication 800-103, 70 pages
(October 2006)

Acknowledgements

The authors, William MacGregor of the National Institute of Standards and Technology (NIST) and William Dutcher and Jamil Khan of Booz Allen Hamilton, wish to thank their colleagues who reviewed drafts of this document and contributed to its development.

Table of Contents

List of Figures

List of Tables

1. Introduction

1.1   Authority

This document has been developed by the National Institute of Standards and Technology (NIST) in furtherance of its statutory responsibilities under the Federal Information Security Management Act (FISMA) of 2002, Public Law 107-347.

NIST is responsible for developing standards and guidelines, including minimum requirements, for providing adequate information security for all agency operations and assets, but such standards and guidelines shall not apply to national security systems. This recommendation is consistent with the requirements of the Office of Management and Budget (OMB) Circular A-130, Section 8b(3), Securing Agency Information Systems, as analyzed in A-130, Appendix IV: Analysis of Key Sections. Supplemental information is provided A-130, Appendix III.

This report has been prepared for use by federal agencies. It may be used by non-governmental organizations on a voluntary basis and is not subject to copyright. Nothing in this document should be taken to contradict standards and guidelines made mandatory and binding on Federal agencies by the Secretary of Commerce under statutory authority. Nor should this report be interpreted as altering or superseding the existing authorities of the Secretary of Commerce, Director of OMB, or any other Federal official.

1.2   Ontology of Identity Defined

"An **ontology** is an explicit specification of a conceptualization. The term is borrowed from philosophy, where Ontology is a systematic account of Existence. For Artificial Intelligence (AI) systems, what "exists" is that which can be represented. When the knowledge of a domain is represented in a declarative formalism, the set of objects that can be represented is called the universe of discourse. This set of objects, and the describable relationships among them, are reflected in the representational vocabulary with which a knowledge-based program represents knowledge. Thus, in the context of AI, we can describe the ontology of a program by defining a set of representational terms. In such an ontology, definitions associate the names of entities in the universe of discourse (e.g., classes, relations, functions, or other objects) with human-readable text describing what the names mean, and formal axioms that constrain the interpretation and well-formed use of these terms. Formally, an ontology is the statement of a logical theory. We use common ontologies to describe *ontological commitments* for a set of agents so that they can communicate about a domain of discourse without necessarily operating on a globally shared theory." [GRUBER]

An ontology of identity credentials, then, is an explicit specification of a conceptualization of identity credentials, including the actors, actions, and objects that establish the relationships of their production, use, and destruction.

or

A definition more applicable to this publication is:

"a description of objects, actors, actions and their relationships within the domain of Identity credentials."

1.3 Purpose

This two-part report describes an ontology of identity credentials, explicitly represented as Extensible Markup Language (XML) schemas, as a framework for retention and exchange of identity credential information.

The primary motivation of this work is to support the requirements of identity credential issuers (e.g., issuers of identity cards, passports, and driver licenses) to manage information about supporting documents and issued credentials.

Supporting documents are of many types and origins. They may be issued by United States (U.S.) national parties, or by international parties. Today, they are usually printed or written documents, and in some cases, the only evidence of issuance may be the hardcopy document itself.

The ontology therefore provides a bridge to the future, a means to represent both identity document content and metadata (i.e., descriptive information) in a standard, electronic form to facilitate automation of identity management systems.

An ontology of identity credentials can be used in many ways. It may be used to:

+ Produce faithful electronic copies of presented identity credentials and documents for archival storage and exchange,

+ Create electronic replica credentials from hardcopy source credentials, and,

+ Create abstracts of electronic credentials that are easy to share and reuse.

A domain ontology can serve these roles because it is more than a data model. An ontology describes the relationships among actors, actions, and objects, and in by so doing, establishes a theory in which all use cases may be expressed.

Note that it is not a goal of this work to specify or design any new kind of identity credential.

1.4 Scope

This report will consider the broadest possible range of identity credentials, and supporting documents insofar as they pertain to identity credential issuance.

Identity credentials are about as commonplace as newsletters, and like newsletters, new credentials are born and old ones fade way. Given such a high rate of change, this ontology of identity credentials must be extensible and open-ended.

Priority will be given to examples of primary and secondary identity credentials (see Section 2.4) issued within the U.S.. These credential types are issued to large populations of subjects, and are used by many relying parties for many applications. Because of the scale of use, they are important in their own right and also important as supporting documents and models for other identity credential systems.

In particular, attention is paid to the supporting document requirements detailed in the U.S. Government I-9 form (http://uscis.gov/graphics/formsfee/forms/files/i-9.pdf).

1.5　Audience and Assumptions

This report is intended for implementers of identity credential issuance and identity management systems with requirements for document retention and exchange. It may also be of value to architects and implementers of other identity-using applications, such as directories and account databases.

This report is issued in two parts. Part 1, Background and Formulation, explores real-world examples of identity credentials and their lifecycles, to extract commonalities and distinctions. Part 2, Specification and Applications, contains the formal XML schemas derived from Part 1 and illustrative applications of the schemas.

1.6　Document Overview

The document is organized as follows:

+ Section 1, *Introduction*, provides the purpose, scope, audience, and assumptions of the document and outlines its structure. This section also defines Identity and related terminology

+ Section 2, *Overview of Identity Concepts*, identifies the characteristics or dimensions of Identity that can be used to categorize credentials

+ Section 3, *The Structure of Credentials*, describes the structure and requirements for physical and logical credentials

+ Section 4, *Survey of Identity Credentials*, this section categorizes key credentials by their purpose e.g. documents for travel and discusses the properties, procedures and inherent issues in using these credentials

+ Section 5, *Identity Credential Standards*, describes and provides references to the most important U.S. standards for primary and secondary identity credentials including some International references

+ Section 6, *Identity Credential System Models*, describes a typical model for credential lifecycle and discusses role of Information Technology (IT) in the lifecycle

+ Section 7, *Trust and Security*, describes how the level of trust in identity credentials is related to the level of security applied to issue the credential, and to authenticate its use.

+ Section 8, *Cases Studies of Identity Documents*, discusses properties and usage of common identity documents

+ Section 9, *Miscellaneous Topics*, discussed related topics that potentially fall under several sections

+ Appendix A, *Acronyms*, contains the list of acronyms used in this document

+ Appendix B, *References*, contains the list of documents that are referred to in this document

+ Appendix C, *Glossary*, contains a list of key definitions referred to or pertinent to this document.

2.   Overview of Identity Concepts

Identity seems simple enough at first. We each have one, it's what makes you "you." The common sense view of identity is the assumption that a living, breathing person has one, exactly one, identity.

Like many words, though, "identity" has different meanings and shadings in different contexts. Here are some alternative perspectives on identity, representing concepts that are commonly regarded as synonymous or overlapping:

+ *Identifiers*: qualities and attributes that name or describe a person.

+ *Memories*: a person's memories of their life experience.

+ *Personality*: a person's recognizable traits and behaviors.

+ *Biology*: a living person with distinctive markers, e.g., Deoxyribo Nucleic Acid (DNA), fingerprints.

+ *Family*: the record of ancestral and descendant relations.

+ *Membership*: belonging to a group or organization.

+ *Citizenship*: civic roles related to voting, international travel, entitlements, taxation, etc.

+ *Business*: relationships as employee, representative, manager.

+ *Religion*: the essential will, soul, or animating spirit.

+ *Culture*: practices and ceremonies of naming.

+ *Law*: a natural person can own property, be charged with a crime, etc.

+ *Reputation*: an individual's public standing in a community.

+ *Agency*: the sequence of actions (track record) performed by one person.

All of these views are important in day-to-day life. They can be loosely grouped as either intrinsic or extrinsic properties. Memories and biology are intrinsic qualities, for example, integral to the human organism. Reputation and agency are extrinsic, they are the external view of how we act and what we do, and thus they require an observer. Intrinsic properties link our past, present, and future, while extrinsic properties, since they must be observed, are necessarily retrospective. In IT terms, for example, we rely on intrinsic properties to design authentication systems (because the systems must authenticate people in the future) and extrinsic properties, often as recorded in logs and audit trails, to establish trustworthiness and accountability.

Identity management and related security goods and services have become a sizable business segment. Why is identity so important? Identity forms the basis for *authorization* and *trust*. A person (a specific identity) is authorized to perform certain actions because an authority trusts them to behave within expectations, e.g., to repay a credit card loan. A person is authorized to possess confidential material with the expectation that they will not disclose it.

Authorization and access control create special challenges for identity management. In typical situations, authorizations are relatively coarse-grained, because the overhead of fine-grained authorizations easily becomes unbearable. For example, an Human Resource (HR) Administrator might be authorized to view any employee's permanent file at any time, even though it would be sufficient to grant authority to view only the files of an assigned division, and these only when an HR action is pending. Authorizations are "larger" than necessary to reduce the number and cost of authorization transactions (frequent verifications and dynamic assignments). This means that not all authorized actions are appropriate, and authorizations are not perfect predictors of good behavior i.e. authorizations are not fully reflective of trust in a particular individual. Authorizations, certificates, and diplomas may have statistical implications, but they are not guarantees.

From the broad perspective of risk management, establishing identity can be considered one element of risk mitigation. Because risk mitigation concerns future actions and events, no strategy is perfect, and the costs of risk mitigation elements should be weighed against the resulting reduction in risk. Useful risk mitigation elements all have operating regions of positive return, break-even points, and regions of negative returns. This is as true of identity management systems as it is of physical access control or network firewalls. Since many enterprise applications and subsystems require registered identities, however, large investments in interoperable identity management systems may yield positive returns.

The first concept of identity listed above is a set of identifiers or attributes. This case is especially important for IT systems, of course, because storing lists of data objects is a fundamental capability of these systems. It is often useful to consider an "on-line" or "network" identity as composed of three parts: 1) a set of identifiers such as Unique Identity (ID) and identifying attributes such as name, address, phone numbers; 2) a set of secrets used for authentication (passwords, pass phrases, Personal Identification Numbers (PIN), and keys); and 3) a set of preferences or personalization profiles for applications (browser home page, application launch bar, etc.). This view expands on identity as a set of qualities, but distinguishes between identifying and non-identifying qualities, and between public and secret identifiers.

This report is about the representation of identity in on-line systems. While it is tempting to concentrate on the on-line concept, the goal of identification and authentication is to bridge the physical world of real people to the on-line world of information. The success of failure of an identity management implementation will depend on its ability to represent the other concepts of identity in an appropriate and effective way.

2.1   Identity Stakeholder Viewpoints

Various stakeholders see identity credentials differently.

An issuer sees risk to reputation (and possibly financial liability) if a credential is issued in a manner contrary to policy. They may also face risk if a credential has been issued in accordance with policy but contains inaccurate information. Issuers often see identity credentials primarily as authorizations.

A relying party sees risk when they accept the assertions made by an identity credential, assigns risk based on that assumption, and either completes or does not complete a transaction based on the assumption. Often, the risk is highest if they complete a fraudulent transaction.

A subject sees risk when they present an identity credential, and either complete or do not complete a transaction. A subject also faces risk from an imposter (commonly called *identity theft*). Often, the greatest risk is failure to complete a transaction due to insufficient trust by the relying party.

An issuer or subject may, in some situations, act as a relying party.

2.2 Identity Credentials

The history of identity credentials is as old as civilization. Identification with a social group is a basic human behavior, and it is often signified by a token or artifact presented to a subject by a group authority. In this sense, a badge, hat, or uniform can be an identity credential: it indicates membership of the wearer in a group.

The earliest forms of written identity documents were probably registers or collections, for the simple reason that few people could write and read. The *Doomsday Book*, produced in England in 1086, registered people and places after the Norman Conquest. Birth, baptismal, and marriage registers expanded and sustained the practice, and in many locales these are the earliest surviving records of the inhabitants.

The need for bearer identity credentials likely arose from two factors: increasing mobility, and improving literacy rates. A letter of safe passage is useful to the traveler if the people they meet can read it. Important credentials, such as university diplomas, have always been produced by the issuer, recorded in a register, and delivered to the subject. Until the 20th century, however, time and distance often made it impossible for a relying party to verify a credential against the issuer's register.

Printed identity credentials identify the issuer and subject and document some qualities or characteristics of the subject, as known to the issuer. Verification of early printed identity credentials was often dependent on recognition of the signature, a seal, or engraving on the document. These processes are error-prone, and identity fraud must have been easy for the well-educated to perpetrate.

In recent years, identity credentials are produced by computer, and the registers of old have become electronic databases. Electronics allows the relying party to examine the database of an issuer without travel, if they are on-line (today, "on-line" means, roughly, connected to the Internet).

Very recently, portable electronic devices have emerged that can store one, a few, or many credentials in electronic form. These range from devices as small as a credit card (i.e., smart cards), to mobile-phone-sized devices or "handhelds", to semi-mobile laptop and desktop computers. Electronic devices can both store a credential and automatically connect to an issuance system to verify electronic credentials, or to request the product of special-purpose credentials for particular transactions.

2.3 Qualities of Identity Credentials

The qualities of identity credentials, as well as the extent to which they add value to the credential vary according to the type of credential. Physical credentials have some characteristics that are different from those of electronic credentials. Identity credentials may have both logical and physical structures that operate either independently or together to validate the credential holder's identity. A logical credential, in order to exist must be presented in some physical form.

This report broadly distinguishes identity credentials from identity documents. Identity documents are any documents that include, reference, or substantiate identity information. Identity credentials are those identity documents whose primary function is to associate a set of attributes with the identifiers of a single subject. A passport or driver license is an example of an identity credential, and an apartment lease or a utility bill is an identity document that is not an identity credential. The process by which a subject proves their Identity is by authentication.

Today, most identity credentials are physical documents, so the characteristics of physical credentials deserve the most attention. In the future, electronic credentials will become more common, but the transition from physical to electronic credentials will still require preservation of the good qualities – and a reduction of the bad qualities – of physical identity credentials.

For both physical and electronic identity credentials, the following *identity document characteristics* can be regarded as good and bad characteristics of those identity documents:

Characteristics of Identity Credentials that are often, but not always, *beneficial* include:

i.   Readily accessible identity information

ii.   Variety of types of identity information

iii.   Irrefutable authentication mechanisms e.g. photograph or biometrics

iv.   Contains biometric info as well as printed data

v.   Resistant to counterfeiting, tampering, or copying

vi.   Protects some data from casual observation

vii.   High degree of trust in the issuer

viii.   Difficulty in obtaining the credential

ix.   Extensive vetting or ID proofing to issue the credential

x.   Recognized, regulated process to apply for and issue credentials

xi.   Durable, low-cost credential medium

xii.   Standardized design, if there are multiple issuing authorities

xiii.   Credential information in a common, widely used language

xiv. Difficult-to-reproduce features

xv.   Credential features signal use restrictions

xvi.   Multiple uses for the same credential

xvii.   Electronic, PIN, or key access to some credential data

xviii.   Additional data ancillary to intended use

xix.   Links to other relevant information, e.g., roles

xx.   Unique credential or user identification number or data key

xxi.   Credential legally belongs to issuer, not to bearer

xxii.   Expired credential seized at renewal

xxiii.   Ability to officially amend credential

Characteristics of Identity Credentials that are often *undesirable* include:

i.   Special equipment required to extract data or use credential

ii. Expensive   credential

iii.   Limited amount of identity information on credential

iv.   Unacceptable privacy violations, avoidable disclosures

v.   Little or no irrefutable identity information

vi.   Few mechanisms against counterfeiting, copying, or tampering

vii.   Credential is easy to acquire, renew, or transfer (few barriers to issue credential)

viii.   Low degree of trust in the credential or the issuer

ix.   Variety of designs, form factors, and media for the same credential e.g. birth certificates)

x.   Frequent changes in format, color, or form factor of document (driver license variations)

xi.   Stickers or attachments to amend credential

xii.   Ability of unauthorized party to amend credential through attachment

xiii.   Multiple uses for the same credential (forged driver license accepted for many other types of transactions)

xiv.   Role-based credentials (not tied to a person)

2.4   Primary, Secondary and Tertiary Identity Credentials

It is useful to group identity credentials into three categories, primary, secondary, and tertiary, because credentials in different categories tend to be created and used differently.

+   **Primary identity credentials** are by-products of significant life events, including birth, marriage, graduation, military entry-on-duty and discharge, and death. Such events are recognized as social occasions requiring ceremony, and are typically witnessed by family, friends, and acquaintances of the subject. In most cases, an original primary identity credential is issued only once per event. A primary identity credential describes the nature, place, and date of the event, and documents event-specific details such as birth weight.

+   **Secondary identity credentials** in contrast, are issued in response to a request for authorization to perform an action (e.g. driver license to operate a vehicle), or demonstrate proof of affiliation (e.g. passport to prove claimed nationality). During a secondary identity credential application process, identity verification relies, to a great degree, on primary and other secondary identity credentials. Personal knowledge of the registrar or trusted third parties may also be relied upon during the application process. Because the application lacks the social context of a primary identity credential, the registrar should take great care to verify the authenticity and accuracy of source documents. Fraudulent births are rare, but fraudulent applications are more common. Secondary identity credentials are often relied upon by law enforcement. Because the consequences of misidentification can be extreme, secondary identity credentials generally include an ID photo and possibly additional biometrics such as fingerprint or signature. Secondary identity credentials are usually government issued, multipurpose, and widely adopted.

+   **Tertiary identity credentials** are issued by an authority or organization for a limited purpose, and include employee badges, membership cards, and loyalty program cards. The identity verification and proofing requirements vary enormously, from almost no requirements (loyalty program cards) to requirements comparable to secondary identity credentials (many employee badges). Tertiary identity cards are rarely multipurpose, and often include no biometric information. Their most common characteristic is an organization-specific unique number. These credentials have a specific lifetime to indicate transient association e.g. visa for a country, travel club membership).

2.5   Owners of Identity Credentials

Identity credentials are often owned by the agency or organization that issued them, not by the person to whom they have been issued. By retaining ownership of a credential, an issuing organization has the right to set conditions on use and to revoke the credential.

Whether the issuing organization can take possession of a revoked credential is another issue. If there is an online system to check the validity or status of credentials, or a list of revoked credentials, that system can be used to check the status of a credential.

For example, a state may revoke a driver license because the holder has accumulated too many points, or if he has been convicted of certain types of driving offenses. In states that have mandatory car insurance laws, the owner of a car that is uninsured may be required to turn in the license plates for the car. In either case, the owner of the car or the holder of the license may decline to surrender either credential. However, if the driver is stopped for a traffic stop, police may check an online system and determine that the car's license plates have been revoked, and the driver's license suspended, and seize both credentials.

Similarly, a U.S. passport legally belongs to the U.S. State Department, which issued the passport. The State Department may revoke the passport that is carried by someone who is declared to be a fugitive, even if he doesn't give up his passport. If he tries to use his passport to enter or leave the U.S., the passport would be seized by U.S. immigration officials.

2.6   Types of Identity Credentials

While we may be accustomed to handling and using only a few identity credentials, there are many variations of those basic documents. For example, the U.S. passport is only one of hundreds of different types of passports in use around the world, and there are several types of U.S. passports. The driver license is a widely used, general-purpose identity document in the U.S., but many people in other countries do not have driver licenses.

Since credentials such as birth certificates and military discharge papers are used for decades, relying parties must be prepared to accept a much greater number of source document types than they may be familiar with.

3. The Structure of Credentials

Someday, we may have completely electronic identities that can replace the physical identity credentials that we use today. But until that day arrives, our identities will be described in paper and plastic documents. In the future, more of those physical documents will contain electronic elements, which may contain digital certificates, digital photographs, fingerprint, DNA, and other biometric files, as well as secure electronic versions of our credential and identity data.

Today, we are at the beginning of a transitional phase that may take us from completely physical to mostly electronic credentials. It is unlikely that we will be able to dispense entirely with physical identity documents. Dispensing with physical documents or credentials entirely requires secure, redundant, failure-resistant on-line systems that use widely available, easy to use, simple, and economical technology. Telephone systems are the only systems that meet most of those criteria, except for security, but it has taken the telephone system more than a hundred years to achieve that level of capability. The Internet meets several of those criteria already, and it holds the most promise for enabling on-line access to identity credentials.

It may be possible for a physical token that has an electronic component, such as a smartcard or a Universal Serial Bus (USB) device, to replace other forms of physical credentials. While that is possible today, the issue is, what is practical?

For the foreseeable future, identity credentials will most likely have both physical and logical components, but the systems in which identity credentials work will evolve. That is, we may see more widespread use of on-line systems to validate the currency or validity of an identity credential, and a move away from static, off-line verification systems. Validating information, such as Public Key Infrastructure (PKI) certificate revocation lists, and credit and identity card revocation or expiration lists, may adopt a decentralized structure, instead of being centralized in one location. In some circumstances, such as for building access, identity credentials may be read by machines more closely than by people. A machine could scan a digitized photograph stored on a credential, and compare it to the facial features of a subject, referring only questionable matches to a guard for closer inspection.

3.1 Logical and Physical Structures of an Identity Credential

Identity credentials may have both physical and logical structures that operate either independently or together to validate the credential holder's identity.

Physical credential structures may include:

+ The dimensions, materials, and layout of the credential

+ Mandatory and optional data elements that are printed or mounted on the credential

+ Special markings, insignia, printing, seals, or features to indicate that the credential is genuine

+ Protective coverings, special printing, watermarks, seals, holographs, coloring or other special physical features to make the credential difficult to counterfeit, copy, or alter

+ Contact or contactless electronic devices, bar codes, magnetic stripes, other machine readable technology, or machine-readable text, to read data stored on the credential

+ A sleeve, shield, cover, or holder to secure or protect the credential, or to prevent the physical or electronic elements of the card from being read or sensed by unauthorized observers

+   Pre-drilled or punched holes, to secure the credential to a lanyard, holder, or a security device

The *logical* features of an identity credential may include:

+   A PIN or password to access secured data or authentication codes (hash, CRC etc)

+   PKI certificates and certificate keys

+   Encryption algorithms used to encrypt or decrypt data or validation sequences

+   Biometric identifiers, such as fingerprint or retinal scan images

+   Digital watermarks

A *digital watermark* modifies digital images or printing on a physical document so that the image or printed parts of the document can carry data. The purpose of the digital watermark is to embed data in a person's photograph on an identity document, or in the body of a document. The data embedded in the digital watermark matches data printed on the document. If the data printed on the document is altered or falsified, it will not match the data in the digital watermark, indicating that the document is suspect.

The digital watermark modifies the image only slightly, so neither the watermark nor the data encoded in it are noticeable to a document examiner. The digital watermark cannot be seen, and a digital watermark cannot be counterfeited without special equipment. However, a high-resolution scanner and a computer running special digital watermark extraction software can extract the digital watermark from the image, read the data, and compare it to the data printed on the document.

Different features of the ID card are utilized in different use cases. Common use cases are, for example:

+   Visual inspection for "introduction" (i.e., examination of personal data relying only on possession, without other authentication)

+   Visual inspection for "authentication" (i.e., authentication using a facial image, signature, or other biometric data, followed by examination of personal data)

+   Photocopying or scanning as documentation of a transaction

+   Automated reading of a Machine Readable Data area (e.g., contactless chip, proximity card, magstripe, 2D barcode, Optical Character Recognition (OCR) text)

+   Authentication via secret marker (e.g., password, secret or private key, or microstructure property of the token)

3.2   Requirements for Logical Structure

An identity credential exists to communicate information to a relying party. To do this, every identity credential has an information model that describes the information that can be conveyed. Logically, the information model is composed of these object identification sections:

+   *Embodiment*: the physical platform or realization of the credential

+   *Issuer*: the issuer of the credential

+   *Subject*: the subject of the credential

+   *Transaction*: transactional information specific to the issued credential

The information model may also contain access control information that applies to the information model as a whole or to parts of the information model.

For example, the logical structure of a Maryland Driver License could be described this way:

Embodiment
- Size
- Material
- Image (images of the obverse and reverse)
- Machine Readable Data
- Tamper Evidence (yes/no result of evaluating tamper-evident features)

Issuer
- Name
- Logo
- Seal
- Graphic
- SignatureImage (image of managers signature)

Subject
- Name
- Address
- SignatureImage
- FacialImage
- Birthdate
- Height
- Weight
- Sex

Transaction
- LicenseNumber
- IssuanceIdentifier
- Issuance Date
- Expiration Date
- Title ("Driver's License")
- Class
- Restrictions
- Type (e.g., "N" means New Resident)
- StandardConditions

The structure of the Maryland Driver's license information model has a simple rationale. The Driver's License has an embodiment, in the form of a plastic object about the size and shape of a credit card. The object is meant to be used in two ways: by direct visual examination (hence the Image attribute), and by reading the Machine Readable Data (which may or may not differ from the legible information on the card). The Embodiment has several tamper-evident features, which when evaluated, communicate that tampering was, or was not, likely done.

In addition to information about the embodiment, the Driver's License is the product of a transaction between the Issuer and the Subject that produced a License. In informational terms, the purpose of the credential is to document the result of the transaction. The information model therefore contains identifiers for the Issuer and the Subject, and attributes and conditions of the license.

The Maryland Driver License is a limited example in one extremely important respect: it is an identity credential that contains only publicly viewable or readable information. An observer, possibly assisted by reading devices, can obtain all of the values in the data model from a Maryland Driver License. A clever observer might use this information to produce a forgery of a Driver License with modified values (because of tamper-resistance features, this is not as easy as it sounds, but forgeries need not be perfect replicas to pass).

It is an important characteristic of many other physical credentials, however, that they contain secrets. Through a process known to an observer, it is possible for the observer to verify that a document does, or does not, contain a secret associated with the credential. Three kinds of secrets can be stored within physical credentials:

i.   Secret passwords or symmetric keys.

ii.   Secret private keys (using Public Key Encryption; see [PKIREF]).

iii.   Properties of credential microstructure that cannot be manufactured.

Cases (i) and (ii) require the identity credential to contain a computer chip. Such credentials are often referred to as "smart cards" or "smart documents". For cases (i) and (ii), the secrets are digital bitstrings that are stored in the memory of the computer chip, and verification of the identity proceeds by a challenge-response protocol. An external observer sends a challenge message to the computer chip, the chip computes a function of the challenge and the secret, and the chip sends the function value to the observer as the response. The observer examines the response to determine if the identity credential is associated with the presenting subject. In case (i), the observer must possess a copy of the secret, locally duplicate the function evaluation, and compare the response from the card to the duplicate. In case (ii), if the private key is generated on the computer chip, it may never be known to an external observer.

Note that case (ii) includes well-known Public Key Encryption algorithms such as RSA and Elliptic Curve, and also less frequently implemented algorithms such as SPEKE and Zero Knowledge Proofs.

For case (iii), the external observer applies some device-assisted scanning process to a presented identity credential. The scanning process is sensitive to some unique qualities of the credential that cannot be manufactured into existence, for example, microscopic surface roughness, or the patterns of wood fibers in paper. The scanned object pattern is matched against a database, and a successful match identifies the credential as a known credential issued to a particular subject. In case (iii), the "secret" is a microscopic, intrinsic property of the credential material that cannot be manufactured.

In terms of the information model, an identity credential has both public and secret attributes. The values of secret attributes cannot be read, although their effect can be observed through challenge-response protocols or special scanning device. Either the generation of the secret is intrinsic to the manufacturing process (e.g. watermark) for the device, or some method is provided to establish a new secret when requested by an external command (e.g. by injecting a secret key).

In the remainder of this report, we will refer to such secrets as *authenticators*. Authenticators are important because they support the authenticity of a credential, and thus the ability of a relying party to infer the identity of the possessor (subject).

The preceding discussion describes authenticators for a physical credential. Semantically, physical credential authenticators are the opposites of tamper evidence: physical credential authenticators provide support for the authenticity of a physical credential, while tamper evidence features provide support for detection of tampering or forgery.

Authenticators may also be present in the logical information model of a credential. Logical credential authenticators support the assertion that some or all of the logical information model was produced, exactly as represented, by the identified issuer. Digital signatures, digital watermarks, and steganography can be applied, for example, to create logical authenticators. Because data structures can be communicated and copied perfectly by digital systems, logical authenticators can support the authorship of information (and by implication, also its integrity), but they cannot support the uniqueness of a logical credential as is done by physical credential authenticators. Physical authenticators cannot support "perfect" integrity of the physical credential (physical objects are subject to wear-and-tear), but logical authenticators can.

The examples of the Maryland Driver License and the other identity documents described in this report provide a basis for the construction of a generalized Identity Document Artifact. The full development of a formal specification of the Identity Document Artifact will be presented in Part 2 of this report. Below, a partial and informal definition of a generalized Identity Document Artifact is presented to illustrate how such a generalization can be constructed. Symbols in boldface are references to constituent definitions.

Any specific instance of the Identity Document Artifact could contain zero or more occurrences of any of the component parts. For example, an ID card could contain no MachineReadableData, or one or more kinds of MachineReadableData. A pure *Electronic ID* (EID) would exist only as a string of bits or bytes, and would thus have LogicalProperties but no meaningful PhysicalProperties except its digital representation in BinaryData of MachineReadableData.

Note that this definition is potentially recursive in two ways. First, as just mentioned, MachineReadableData could contain an EID, which could contain further EIDs, this being simple recursive embedding of data objects. Each of these embedded objects could, itself, be described as an Identity Document Artifact. This structuring is necessary, for example, to describe the structure of digitally signed objects such as certificates, because they contain signatures that may themselves contain additional certificates. The Identity Document Artifact can also be recursive in the physical space, through physical attachments such as seals or endorsements that are themselves identity documents.

Machine readable data on an identity credential may also be encrypted, in order to protect it from inadvertent disclosure, or to maintain its integrity. For example, a passport that has a contactless chip embedded in it may have the passport number, the holder's name and birthdate, passport expiration date, and other information stored on the chip. To prevent this data from being read without the passport holder's knowledge, the data on the chip will most likely be encrypted, or protected by some electronic method.

As desirable as it may seem to encrypt data on a credential, encryption presents its own set of challenges. Encryption increases the credential overhead required for storage and processing. Encryption algorithms utilize a unique private encryption and decryption key for each credential. In the case of encrypted passport fields, there would be a requirement for each passport to use its own unique encryption key to encrypt and decrypt the data. Using a single key for all passports, or a single key to encrypt data on a block of passports, would leave the data available to anyone who had the key.

Normalization (i.e., the establishment of constraints, possibly interdependent, on the value sets of attributes) is not addressed in this definition below. In the full development, it will be necessary to identify normalization constraints as artifacts within the model. This will allow, for example, the description of an original identity document with an unnormalized "State" attribute, with an amendment issued by another party, containing a normalized "State" attribute restricted to the two-letter U.S. postal abbreviations for states. Normalization will also accomplish natural language and alphabet selection, where these are meaningful.

Defn: Identity Document Artifact
 PhysicalProperties

> **GrossPhysicalProperties**
> **VisibleImage**
> **MachineReadableData**

 Authenticator

> **TamperEvidence**
> **Attachment**

 LogicalProperties

> **Issuer**
> **Subject**
> **Transaction**

 Authenticator

> **AnnotationOrAmendment**

Defn: GrossPhysicalProperties
> Material
> Shape
> Size
> Weight
> Surfaces
> Folding

Defn: VisibleImage
 Obverse
 Reverse
 Page
 Tile

Defn: MachineReadableData
 ReadMethod
 BinaryData
 QualityMethod
 Quality

Defn: Attachment
> Attachment Method
 Position
> **Identity Document Artifact**

Defn: TamperEvidence
 Feature
 Identifier
 TamperEstimate

Defn: Issuer *or* Subject
 Name
 Organization
 Title
 Address
 Birthdate
 Height
 Weight
 Gender
 FacialImage
 SignatureImage
 MarqueImage
 TelephoneNumber
 FaxNumber
 EmailAddress
 WebAddress

Defn: Transaction
 Title
 Subtitle
 Form
 Identifier
 Date
        Place
 Expires
 Conditions

Defn: AnnotationOrAmendment
 Method
 Content

3.3   Requirements for Physical Structure

The *physical* structure of a credential refers to the following characteristics of the credential:

+ Material or medium

+ Layout of identity elements on the credential

+ Dimensions

+ Integrated security features

+ Machine readable technologies

For example, a typical user might see or feel that a smart card is the same size as a credit card, and that it is composed of plastic. But they won't know what kind of plastic, or whether it contains an embedded contactless chip. Those facts require different kinds of observations.

3.4   Inconsistency of Information

Despite the best intentions and diligent efforts of the issuer, the information communicated by an identity credential may not be entirely accurate, internally consistent, or unambiguous within a particular context.

Errors-in-fact may be introduced during the credential issuance process making an issued credential inaccurate in some respect. This is more likely if the subject does not have the opportunity to verify the on-line information prior to production of the identity credential. An incorrect birth date is an example.

Information on an identity credential may be inconsistent in minor or major respects. Inconsistencies can arise when attribute values are redundantly represented, for example, printed on an ID card and recorded on an embedded chip or magstripe. Minor inconsistencies are generally representational differences that would be ignored by a human examiner, for example, "William I MacGregor" versus "William I. MacGregor". Major inconsistencies are direct conflicts that cannot be decided without an authoritative external source, for example, "DL #1234" versus "DL #1235". Inconsistencies may also arise indirectly when data violates an integrity assertion, for example, "the birth date should precede the issuance data."

Some ambiguity or uncertainty is unavoidable in any use of language. In an identity credential, however, the problem is magnified because the number of utterances is small and fixed. Within a large population, many names are highly ambiguous. The temporal ordering of two birthdates, for example, can depend on the places of birth. Uncertainty may be reduced by requiring data values to be normalized, or selected from a pre-defined set, for example, "Universal Time Coordinated (UTC) time and date represented according to ISO 8601", or Zip Codes selected from a published list. Normalization makes matching against values easier, and facilitates inference about data values such as determining the ordering of events.

With regard to electronic replicas for existing credentials, in this section we note these principles:

    i.   since errors-in-fact, inconsistencies, and ambiguities all exist in source documents, they will exist in faithful electronic replicas, too;

   ii.   inconsistencies arise from redundancy and violations of integrity assertions;

  iii.   normalization of an attribute's value set is an act of authorship, whether on the part of the issuer, or as an amendment after credential issuance.

4.　Survey of Identity Credentials

This section categorizes key credentials by their purpose, e.g. documents for travel, and discusses the properties, procedures and inherent issues in using these credentials.

Identity documents may be categorized in two broad areas: the circumstances under which they were issued, or the purpose for which they are used. Table 1 attempts to categorize identity documents in eleven different categories, each of which falls into the circumstances of issue or purpose of use categories.

Many identity documents can be classified in more than one category, particularly if the document has a number of uses. For example, a driver license is a privilege document, in that its primary purpose is to indicate that the holder has met the qualifications for the privilege of driving a motor vehicle. It is also widely used in the U.S. as a general-purpose identity document, and an identity document for domestic travel and transportation. It may also be accepted for building access as a guest, if only to establish the identity of the person to whom building access is being granted.

Some examples of documents that fall into each of these categories are specified in Table 1. Documents marked with an asterisk (*) have been listed previously, as they fall into more than one category.

Table 1:　Categories of Identity Documents and Examples

Category	Description	Examples of Documents
Identity	Documents that are issued for a specific purpose, such as a driver license, but that are generally used a secondary identity credentials.	Driver license Government (federal, state, or local) employee ID card Military ID card PKI Identity certificate
Entitlement	Documents that indicate that the holder is eligible for a service or benefit, such as health care.	Medicare/health insurance enrollment card Food Stamp Eligibility card Public Assistance Eligibility card Military family member ID Native American tribal document (various, if issued by tribe or Bureau of Indian Affairs) Veteran's benefit ID card Letter of Authorization for Post Exchange or Base Exchange privileges and gas ration coupons
Privilege	Documents that indicate that the holder has qualified to exercise a privilege, such as driving a type of motor vehicle.	Driver license * Vehicle registration and license plates Power of attorney Professional license Professional accreditation certificate Resident Alien Registration card Voter registration Permit to carry a firearm

Category	Description	Examples of Documents
Transportation and Travel	Documents that serve as identification for travel, which is required by airlines, immigration, or customs officials, such as a passport.	U.S. passport Foreign passport Airline boarding pass Re-entry Permit/I-327 U.S. visa Refugee document
Life Event	Documents issued at the time of significant life events, such as birth, marriage, divorce, or death.	Birth certificate Marriage certificate Marriage license Divorce decree Separation agreement Death certificate Graduation certificate or degree
Employment Eligibility	Documents that indicate that the holder is eligible to be legally employed.	Social Security card Resident Alien Registration Card * Employment Authorization Card (INS Form 688A/B)
Employment Verification	Documents that verify that a person is employed, although they may not indicate if the employment is legal or illegal	Company employee ID Government employee ID Public Safety employee ID Military ID * W-2 Form
Building Access	Documents that grant the holder access to buildings or facilities.	Company ID card * Federal ID card Military ID card * School ID card
Citizenship	Documents that assert the holder's citizenship.	Passport (U.S. or foreign) * Certificate of Naturalization Certificate of Foreign Birth Abroad U.S. Citizen ID Card (INS Form I-197)
Financial and Credit	Documents that establish identity in order to establish bank accounts, to maintain tax records, and perform other financial transactions.	Bank account statement Checking account statement Mutual fund investment account Brokerage account Margin account Credit card Line of credit Mortgage loan Vehicle title Property deed Estate executor agreement Trustee agreement
Obligation	Documents that indicate that the holder is required to perform some kind of obligation, such as military service.	Selective Service registration Organ donor card Military commission Military enlistment document

4.1   I-9 Documents

In 1986, as part of the Immigration Reform and Control Act, the U.S. Immigration and Naturalization Service (INS) issued a list of identity documents that could be used to establish identity, citizenship, and the right to work legally in the U.S.. This list, referred to as the I-9 list for the INS I-9 form, is supposed to be used by prospective employers to determine if a person could be legally employed.

At that time, as now, illegal immigration was a serious problem. The purpose of the I-9 form was to require employers to verify the identity of a job applicant, and, more important, that the applicant had the right to work in the U.S.. Under federal law, illegal aliens, or visitors whose visas do not permit them to work while in the U.S., are not permitted to be employed in the U.S. U.S. citizens and non U.S. citizens with work authorizations, however, are eligible to work. The I-9 Employment Eligibility Verification form is completed by both the applicant and the employer. It is the employer's record of their basis for determining eligibility of an employee to work in the U.S.. The current version of the I-9 form is at http://uscis.gov/graphics/formsfee/forms/files/i-9.pdf and lists 29 documents that can be used for identity and/or employment eligibility.

Some of the key documents acceptable for employment are summarized in Table 2:

Table 2: I-9 Summary of Lists of Acceptable Documents

and Employment Eligibility	Identity	
U.S. Passport (unexpired or expired)	Drivers License or State/territory/government agency issued ID with photograph and details similar to driver's license	U.S. SSN (other than card stating that it is not valid for employment)
Certificate of U.S. Citizenship	School Id card (with photograph)	Certification of birth abroad
Certificate of Naturalization	Voter registration card	Original or certified copy of a U.S. birth certificate
Foreign passport (unexpired) with valid employment authorization	U.S. military card or draft record	Native American tribal document
Resident Alien Registration Card (Green card)	Military family member's ID card	U.S. citizen ID card
Temporary resident card	U.S. coast guard merchant marine card	ID card for use of resident citizen in the U.S.A
Employment authorization card	Native American tribal document	Employment authorization document issued by Department of Homeland Security (other than those listed under List A)

and Employment Eligibility	Identity	
Reentry permit	School, day-care or nursery record or report card (for persons under 18 who are unable to produce above documents)	
Refugee travel document	Clinic, doctor or hospital record (for persons under 18 who are unable to produce above documents)	

The I-9 document lists the types of documents that a job applicant must present to a prospective employer to verify his or her identity and employment eligibility. Some documents, such as a U.S. Passport, are acceptable to establish both the applicant's identity and U.S. citizenship, which make the applicant eligible to be legally employed.

Two other lists of documents specify documents that may be used to establish identity and employment eligibility separately, if the applicant does not have a document like a passport that establishes both. A driver license, for example, is an acceptable I-9 document to establish identity. A Social Security card establishes employment eligibility, provided it is not marked "Not Valid for Employment".

In 1991, the INS modified the list of I-9 documents, eliminating many of the documents that established both the applicant's identity eligibility to be legally employed. However, printed and on-line copies of the I-9 form still contain the original list of documents.

Just because an applicant presents identity documents specified in the I-9 lists does not mean that the individual is actually eligible to work. The documents presented, specifically driver licenses and Social Security cards, may be counterfeit. It is up to the employer to determine if the documents are genuine. Many employers, particularly employers of seasonal agricultural workers, are under more pressure to plant, cultivate, and harvest crops than they are to check the authenticity of identity documents.

5.   Identity Credential Standards and Organizations

This section briefly describes the most important U.S. standards for Identity and the organizations behind these standards.

5.1   National Center for Health Statistics – Vital Statistics Standards

The National Vital Statistics System is the oldest and most successful example of inter-governmental data sharing in Public Health and the shared relationships, standards, and procedures form the mechanism by which National Center for Health Statistics (NCHS) collects and disseminates the Nation's official vital statistics. These data are provided through contracts between NCHS and vital registration systems operated in the various jurisdictions legally responsible for the registration of vital events – births, deaths, marriages, divorces, and fetal deaths. In the U.S., legal authority for the registration of these events resides individually with the 50 States, 2 cities (Washington, DC, and New York City), and 5 territories (Puerto Rico, the Virgin Islands, Guam, American Samoa, and the Commonwealth of the Northern Mariana Islands). These jurisdictions are responsible for maintaining registries of vital events and for issuing copies of birth, marriage, divorce, and death certificates.

Standard forms for the collection of the data and model procedures for the uniform registration of the events are developed and recommended for nationwide use through cooperative activities of the jurisdictions and NCHS.

Center for Disease Control's National Center for Health Statistics is working with State partners represented by the National Association of Public Health Statistics and Information Systems (NAPHSIS) and the Social Security Administration to fundamentally re-engineer the processes through which vital statistics are produced in the U.S., including implementation of the 2003 revised certificates. The primary objective is to improve the timeliness, quality, and sustainability of the decentralized vital statistics system, along with collection of the revised and new content of the 2003 certificates, by adopting technologically sophisticated yet cost-effective model IT systems based on nationally developed standards and models. Information on the re-engineering activities and technical documents are available at the NAPHSIS web site [http://www.naphsis.org/], as well as at the NCHS certificate revision web site [http://www.cdc.gov/nchs].

5.2   International Civil Aviation Organization

One of International Civil Aviation Organization's (ICAO) chief activities is standardization, the establishment of International Standards, Recommended Practices and Procedures covering the technical fields of aviation: licensing of personnel, rules of the air, aeronautical meteorology, aeronautical charts, units of measurement, operation of aircraft, nationality and registration marks, airworthiness, aeronautical telecommunications, air traffic services, search and rescue, aircraft accident investigation, aerodromes, aeronautical information services, aircraft noise and engine missions, security and the safe transport of dangerous goods. After a Standard is adopted it is put into effect by each ICAO Contracting State in its own territories. As aviation technology continues to develop rapidly, the Standards are kept under constant review and amended as necessary.

For further information see www.icao.int.

5.2.1   Machine Readable Travel Documents

Building on its expertise in setting standards for globally interoperable systems, ICAO also plays a key role in the area of Machine Readable Travel Documents (MRTDs) and biometric enhancement of MRTDs.

An *ePassport* is a machine-readable document which contains a person's information and photograph printed on a laminated plastic card. The plastic card itself contains a chip which is able to store data in electronic form, including one of several embedded biometric information options such as a fingerprint, facial recognition or iris scan.

The ICAO has developed and published a set of standards for the production of electronic passports. In addition, the U.S. Department of State Under the Patriot Act, from October 26, 2004 forward all individuals traveling from one of 27 countries covered under the Visa Waiver Act are required to have a "Machine-Readable Passport" with biometric identifier, usually referred to as an electronic passport or ePassport.

5.2.2   The New Technologies Working Group

The New Technologies Working Group (NTWG) is responsible for research, analysis and reporting on new technologies available today or in the future for use in MRTDs. The Group's current emphasis is on document security. The NTWG acts as a forum for presentation of candidate technologies, including chips, bar-code, optical memory storage as well as the confirmation of identity with biometrics. In addition, the NTWG seeks input with respect to machine authentication and security features for documents.

5.3   The Initiative for Open Authentication

Open Authentication (OATH) is an organization that includes powerful high-tech players such as IBM, VeriSign, and the Smart Card Alliance. They are working to address some of the major challenges facing networked entities. The three major challenges include:

i.   Theft of or unauthorized access to confidential data

ii.   The inability to share data over a network without an increased security risk limits the ability of organizations to conduct business in the most efficient way.

iii. The lack of a viable single sign-on framework is inhibiting the growth of electronic commerce and networked operations.

5.3.1   Personal Strong Authentication

The Initiative for OATH addresses these challenges with standard, open technology that is available to all. OATH is taking an all-encompassing approach, delivering solutions that allow for strong authentication of all users on all devices, across all networks. One of OATH's major accomplishment was the endorsement of a formal standard (October, 2004 [http://openauthentication.org/pr_04_10_26_1.asp] for the calculation of one-time passwords (OTP).

OTP would be useless to any hackers who successfully eavesdropped on a computer session. As a result, OTP will probably be the first part of OATH's vision to be widely adopted to strengthen authentication. OATH is also working with internet standards bodies such as the Internet Engineering Task Force (IETF) on other approaches such as challenge/response authentication, in which a remote server establishes a communications session to verify the physical device a user is carrying, and PKI, involving the deployment of hard-to-fake digital signatures.

5.4   The Internet Engineering Task Force

IETF is a large open international community of network designers, operators, vendors, and researchers concerned with the evolution of the Internet architecture and the smooth operation of the Internet. It is open to any interested individual.

The actual technical work of the IETF is done in its working groups, which are organized by topic into several areas (e.g., routing, transport, security, etc.). The IETF working groups are grouped into areas, and managed by Area Directors who are members of the Internet Engineering Steering Group (IESG). Providing architectural oversight is the Internet Architecture Board, (IAB). The IAB also adjudicates appeals when someone complains that the IESG has failed. The IAB and IESG are chartered by the Internet Society (ISOC) for these purposes.

The Internet Assigned Numbers Authority (IANA) is the central coordinator for the assignment of unique parameter values for Internet protocols. The IANA is chartered by ISOC to act as the clearinghouse to assign and coordinate the use of numerous Internet protocol parameters.

5.4.1   vCard

vCard is the electronic business card. It is a powerful new means of Personal Data Interchange (PDI) that is automating the traditional business card. Whether it's your computer (hand held organizer, Personal Information Manager (PIM), electronic email application, Web Browser) or telephone, the vCard is increasingly revolutionizing one's personal communications.

Some of vCard features include:

+   vCards carry vital directory information such as name, addresses (business, home, mailing, parcel), telephone numbers (home, business, fax, pager, cellular, voice, data, video), email addresses and Internet Universal Resource Locators (URL).

+   vCards can also have graphics and multimedia including photographs, company logos, audio clips such as for name pronunciation

+   geographic and time zone information in vCards lets others know when to contact you.

+   vCards support multiple languages

+   the vCard spec is transport and operating system independent so you can have vCard-ready software on any computer

+   vCards are Internet friendly, standards based, and have wide industry support.

Some of the ways vCards are being used include:

+   infrared Exchange

+   internet Mail

+   computer/telephony applications

+   video and data conferencing

The scenarios outlined above are $_{now}$ becoming a reality with the $_{vCard\ V2.1\ Specification}$ from the Internet Mail Consortium and the $_{vCard\ V3.0\ Specification}$ approved as a proposed standard by the IETF. These specifications were developed in cooperation with leading producers of desktop software (PIMs, telephony products), hand-held organizers, Internet web clients, Email systems, on-line information and directory services, and other interested parties. In fact, the vCard technology has already been adopted by many of these vendors who are now incorporating it into their products.

5.5   The American Association of Motor Vehicle Administrators

American Association of Motor Vehicle Administrators (AAMVA) is a tax-exempt, nonprofit organization striving to develop model programs in motor vehicle administration, police traffic services and highway safety. The association serves as an information clearinghouse for these same disciplines, and acts as the international spokesman for these interests. Founded in 1933, AAMVA is a voluntary, nonprofit, tax exempt, educational organization. AAMVA represents the state and provincial officials in the U.S. and Canada who administer and enforce motor vehicle laws.

5.5.1   DL/ID Security Framework

The association's programs encourage uniformity and reciprocity among the states and provinces, and liaisons with other levels of government and the private sector. Its program development and research activities provide guidelines for more effective public service.

AAMVA determined the need for a comprehensive framework of minimum requirements with enhanced recommendations to improve the quality, reliability, uniformity and security of the driver licensing process in North America. As a result, AAMVA compiled and produced its Driver's License and Personal Identification (*DL/ID*) *Security Framework: A Package of Decisions Based on Best Practices, Standards, Specifications and Recommendations to Enhance Driver's License Administration and Identification Security.*

AAMVA's role in the implementation of the Real ID Act (see Section 5.8.1) will be to:

+ leverage experience gained in developing the AAMVA DL/ID Security Framework and the Driver License Agreement to develop recommendations for effective regulations

+ establish clear assumptions that allow each jurisdiction to more accurately assess the impact of implementing the REAL ID Act requirements

+ ensure practical and effective implementation of the REAL ID Act

+ assist in and support the creation of common system infrastructures that address the verification requirements of the REAL ID Act

5.6   Organization for the Advancement of Structured Information Standards

Organization for the Advancement of Structured Information Standards (OASIS) is a not-for-profit, international consortium that drives the development, convergence, and adoption of e-business standards. The consortium produces Web services standards along with standards for security, e-business, and standardization efforts in the public sector and for application-specific markets. Founded in 1993, OASIS has more than 5,000 participants representing over 600 organizations and individual members in 100 countries.

The Consortium hosts two of the most widely respected information portals on XML and Web services standards, Cover Pages and XML.org. OASIS Member Sections include Computer Graphics Metafile Open, DCML, LegalXML, PKI, and Universal Description, Discovery and Integration (UDDI).

5.6.1   Standard Generalized Markup Language Open

OASIS was founded in 1993 under the name Standard Generalized Markup Language (SGML) Open as a consortium of vendors and users devoted to developing guidelines for interoperability among products that support the SGML. OASIS changed its name in 1998 to reflect an expanded scope of technical work, including the XML and other related standards.

5.7 Liberty Alliance, OASIS − Federated ID

Federated Id is a system that allows individuals to use the same user name, password or other personal identification to sign on to the networks of more than one enterprise in order to conduct transactions. Partners in a Federated Identity Management (FIM) system depend on each other to authenticate their respective users and vouch for their access to services. That allows, for example, a sales representative to update an internal forecast by pulling information from a supplier's database, hosted on the supplier's network.

Federated Id has become necessary so that companies can cost effectively share applications without needing to adopt the same technologies for directory services, security and authentication. Within companies, directory services such as Microsoft's Active Directory or products using the Lightweight Directory Access Protocol have allowed companies to recognize their users through a single identity. But asking multiple companies to match up technologies or maintain full user accounts for their partners' employees is unwieldy. FIM allows companies to keep their own directories and securely exchange information from them.

How does it work? A company must trust its FIM system partners to vouch for their users. Each participant must rely on each partner to say, in effect, "This user is OK; let them access this application." Partners also need a standard way to send that message, such as one that uses the conventions of the Security Assertion Markup Language (SAML). SAML allows instant recognition of whether the prospective user is a person or a machine, and what that person or machine can access. SAML documents can be wrapped in a Simple Object Access Protocol (SOAP) message for the computer-to-computer communications needed for Web services. Or they may be passed between Web servers of federated organizations that share live services.

Who is using it? Early adopters include American Express, Boeing, General Motors, and Nokia. Another, Proctor & Gamble, had improvised its own federated-identity system using the more generic eXtensible Markup Language, but is now moving to adopt SAML.

Are the standards solid? They're getting there. SAML is backed by **OASIS**. The **Liberty Alliance,** an industry group formed to promote federated-identity standards, has adopted SAML 1.1 as part of its application framework. Microsoft and IBM have proposed an alternative specification called WS-Security. But some technology analysts believe that OASIS may try to make these two approaches converge in SAML 2.0.

What are the challenges? Trusting a partner to authenticate its own users is a good thing only if that partner has solid security and user-management practices. Also, while some Web access-management products now support SAML, implementing the technology still commonly requires customization to integrate applications and develop user interfaces.

5.8 Legislative Bearings on Identity Standards

This section describes the main legislative bearings on ID standards in the U.S.A, such as the Real ID Act.

5.8.1 Real ID Act

The *Real ID* Act was signed into law by in May 2005 requiring all U.S. jurisdictions to follow new DL/ID cards issuance and document standards. The intent of the Act is to create documents that are acceptable for official federal purposes (e.g., boarding an airplane or entering federal facilities). Moreover, further intent is to improve security and to improve assurance that credential was issued by a reliable source The Act sets minimum standards for the creation and issuance of the documents by motor vehicle agencies. A rulemaking process by the Department of Homeland Security will further define the minimum standards set in the Act.

6.　Identity Credential System Models

This section introduces a set of models or "planes" representing different projections of the Identity Credential Ontology.

6.1　The Actor Plane

The Actor Plane describes the most significant actors and relationships in the domain of identity credential systems. The actors named in this plane perform the mainstream actions that justify the existence of the identity credential system.

The Issuing Authority issues credentials and updates credential status after issuance. A credential is issued to the Subject of the credential, who takes physical possession of it. The Subject presents a credential to a relying party for examination in the course of a transaction between the Subject and Relying Party. The Relying Party validates the credential through a Validation Service that returns the status of the credential as updated by the Issuing Authority, and the Relying Party uses the information that was validated. The Relying Party will forward information about the transaction to one or more Transaction Intermediaries. The Subject, Relying Party, and Transaction Intermediaries may engage in dispute resolution through a Judicial Authority.

Many less frequent relationships are not shown here. For example, any party may act as a Relying Party to the extent that they use an identity credential. A Judicial Authority will likely use services of the Issuing Authority and/or Validation Services during dispute resolution.

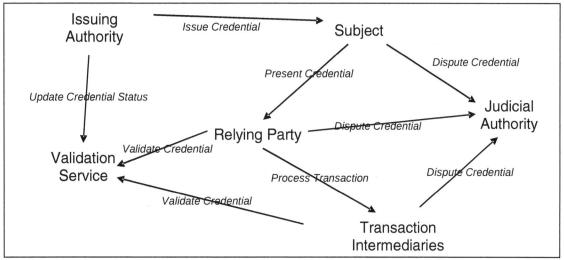

Figure 1:　The Actor Plane

6.2　The Issuance Plane

The Issuing Authority is the center point of identity credential issuance. The Issuance Plane describes the relationships between the Issuing Authority and other parties that are relevant to identity credential issuance, but it does not describe a specific workflow or sequencing.

The Applicant makes application to the Issuing Authority to obtain an identity credential. Typically, the Applicant is also the Subject, who receives the issued credential. However, the Applicant could be the Sponsor, who approves issuance of the credential, in cases where the credential is automatically issued to the subject. The Issuing Authority obtains supporting information from multiple sources, including the

Applicant, Investigation Services, and References (often named in the application). From the Enrollment Service, the Issuing Authority receives biometric bindings (e.g., ID photo, fingerprints, or iris templates) of applicant biometrics to the application workflow record. The Issuing Authority delivers the issued credential to the Subject, and may provide issuance notifications to Relying Organizations, as well as an initial status update to one or more Validation Services.

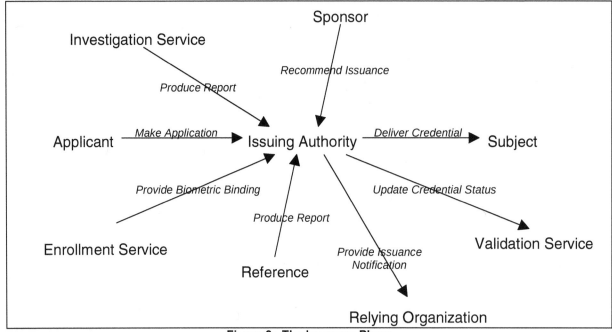

Figure 2: The Issuance Plane

6.3   The Maintenance Plane

The Maintenance Plane describes relationships of the Issuing Authority with other parties after issuance of an identity credential.

The Issuing Authority may provide status updates to Relying Parties (including the Subject) and Validation Service, including notices of credential termination. The Subject or the Sponsor may request the Issuing Authority to make credential changes. The Issuing Authority interacts with the Credential in order to perform updates, including termination, renewal, suspension/resumption, and modification.

Identity Credentials can be considered either "active" or "passive". Active credentials can participate in protocols as agents, and can modify their own stored state at the request of the Issuing Authority. Passive credentials are not capable of modification on request, and for the Issuing Authority to "change" a passive credential it must produce and deliver a new identity credential with the desired characteristics, and terminate the old credential.

Note that a credential may be terminated without updating the credential itself. This is normally done with a lost or stolen credential. In this case, Relying Parties and Validation Services may still be notified of the termination.

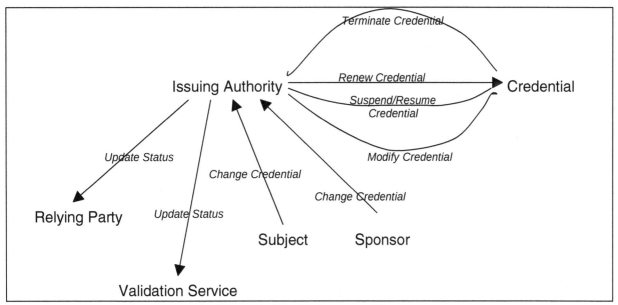

Figure 3: The Maintenance Plane

6.4   The Transaction Plane

The Transaction Plane describes the use of an identity credential in a transaction between the Subject and a Relying Party.

The Subject presents the identity credential to the Relying Party, and typically receives a receipt from the Relying Party containing information from the identity credential, during the transaction. The Relying Party combines information from the identity credential with other transaction-relevant information, and communicates a transaction record to a Transaction Intermediary. The first Transaction Intermediary may forward the transaction record, or structures derived from it, through several additional Transaction Intermediaries. These Transaction Intermediaries may, typically at a later time, produce reports on the transaction that are returned to the Subject, the Relying Party engaged in the transaction, and in some cases additional Relying Parties.

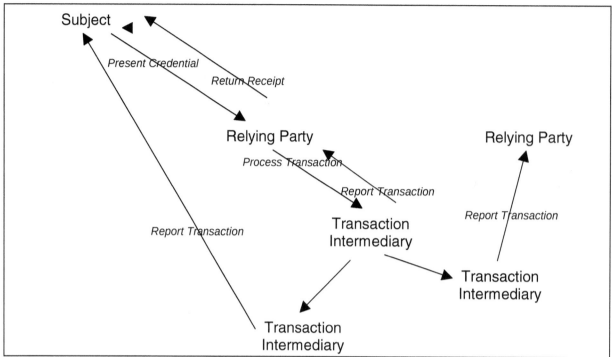

Figure 4: The Transaction Plane

6.5 Life Events Plane

The Life Events Plane illustrates events in the life of a Subject that might cause primary identity credentials, secondary identity credentials, or other identity documents to be produced. Primary identity credentials include the Subject's Birth and Death Certificates, Diplomas, and Marriage Certificate. Secondary identity credentials are requested by the Subject and supported by primary identity and other secondary identity credentials. Important examples include Driver Licenses, Passports, and Voter Registration Cards. Identity documents are specific to the Subject, contain Personally Identifiable Information, and are widely recognized as documents of record. Identity documents generally lack, however, the characteristics of general utility, durability, tamper-resistance, and compact size that are characteristic of identity credentials. Examples include tax returns, health and real estate records.

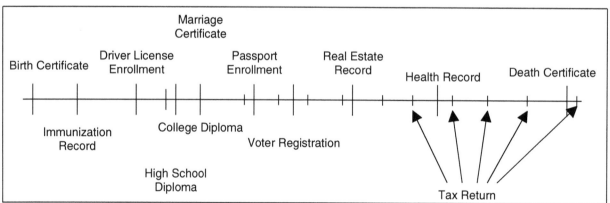

Figure 5: Life Events Plane

7. Trust and Security

Identity credentials are useful only to the extent that:

+ Someone who examines the credential agrees that the credential holder is indeed the person described on the credential

+ The examiner accepts the credential as authentic, genuine, and reliable

+ The examiner accepts the assertion being made by the credential.

These decisions depend on the examiner's ability to authenticate the credential, the holder, and the credential assertion. Some parts of the authentication process are subjective, and some are objective.

For example, an electronic credential, such as a PKI certificate, is usually evaluated objectively. Some types of PKI certificates are issued only after a rigorous identity verification process, so the person who presents the certificate is assumed to be that person. An examiner may evaluate an identity document itself subjectively. Despite the identity claim evidenced on a birth certificate, an examiner may evaluate the credential based on how authentic the document seems. If the document is a photocopy of an original document, if it does not have an embossed seal, or if the document appears to have been altered or forged, the examiner may reject the document as not authentic.

Subject authentication, which is the acceptance of the identity or assertion made by a credential, involves authentication of the credential holder, as well as the credential itself. Identity credentials are only as good as the willingness of an examiner to accept them, and to agree to the authenticity of the claims they make about the holder's identity.

7.1 Security Objectives

The primary security objectives for identity credentials at the point of use are:

+ *Provenance*: was the card issued by the indicated, legitimate authority?

+ *Identification*: what symbols on the card identify the subject?

+ *Validation*: does the authority still consider the card valid?

+ *Authentication*: is the person presenting the card its subject?

+ *Authorization*: does the card grant relevant permissions to the subject?

Each of these five objectives can be achieved through one set of mechanisms for the physical model of a credential, and another set for the logical information model. Visual indication of provenance, for example, might be supported by the issuer's seal or logo printed on the physical card, covered by a tamper-evident laminate. Logical provenance might be assured through a digital signature on the credential's information model.

Other security objectives can be discerned in an application or systems view of identity credentials. For example, security objectives arise from a need to protect the issuer's processes and databases.

7.2 Identity Credential Security

Issuing authorities recognize that identity credentials or documents must incorporate features or capabilities that assure the security and authenticity of the credential or document. These measures may include special printing, difficult-to-reproduce colors, watermarks, and designs, holograms and Kinegrams, digital printing, special paper or media, lamination, and electronic data elements.

Even if they cannot assure that a document or credential cannot be duplicated or forged, issuing authorities must make it difficult or expensive to do so. The degree of difficulty to reproduce or forge a document or credential is part of its security model. A credential's security model may include some or all of the following elements:

+ High-assurance identity verification process before issuing the credential

+ Type and extent of identifying data on the credential

+ Special document media, printing, or features

+ Various printing techniques used on the same document

+ Electronically-readable devices, such as integrated circuits, bar codes, or mag stripes

+ Ultraviolet and infrared light visible inks

+ Security threads, latent images, optically-variable marking, high-reflection foil, iridescent coatings, microtext, see-through images, overprinting, watermarking, or patterned laminating

+ Additional data embedded electronically in the document that is not printed on the document

+ Hidden data elements that verify data printed on the document (digital watermarks)

+ Biometric data, such as fingerprints or retinal scan information

+ Verification data printed on another part of the document (credit card verifying codes)

+ Electronically-duplicated visual data (printed photograph and digital photo image on document)

+ PKI certificates or digitally-signed credentials

+ Digitally-signed or encrypted data on the credential

+ External services or on-line databases to verify credential information

+ External services or on-line databases to identify revoked or invalid credentials

+ Readily verifiable identity information, such as a photograph

+ Visually noticeable differences among similar credentials (portrait vs. landscape orientation for driver licenses for people under 21)

+ Specially-laminated or permanently sealed documents

+ Polycarbonate composite document data pages

+ Foil overlays or embossing, particularly over several parts of the credential

+ Centralized, delayed production and delivery vs. over-the-counter credential production

+ Credential expiration periods

+ Revocation or destruction of an expired credential

Each of the five identity credentials described in Section 9 (a U.S. driver license, U.S. passport, birth certificate, Social Security card, Personal Identity Verification (PIV) card) has its own security model, which are described in the appropriate sub-sections of section 9. The security model is evaluated according to four criteria: identity verification, credential production, and credential maintenance and credential termination.

Table 3 maps some of these security measures against the security objectives they seek to achieve. Note that some of these methods protect the credential, and some protect the information on the credential. Different credential protection methods can help achieve different types of security objectives.

Table 3: Mapping of Security Measures and Objectives

Security Method	and anti-disclosure)	Integrity (anti-tampering)	counterfeiting)
Digital watermarks		x	x
Optical variable devices			x
Special or controlled media	x		x
Digital signatures		x	x
Smart card access controls	x X		
Encryption x			
Document security lamination	X		

7.3   Methods Used to Authenticate a Person

Some of the methods that are used to authenticate a person include:

+ **Visual Identification.** Obviously, visual authentication is easiest and most reliable when the identification credential includes a photograph. Depending on the age of the photograph, the holder of the credential may look somewhat different to an examiner, but the holder should closely resemble the individual depicted in the photo. Now that most states require photos on driver licenses, and the driver license has become the de facto general-purpose identity credential, this government-issued photo ID is both universally used and accepted.

+ **Identity Information Verification.** Even if the holder looks like the person in the photograph, an examiner may use other information on the credential to authenticate the credential holder further. For example, the holder's birth date is a standard data element on a driver license. An examiner could ask the credential holder to cite his birthday and verify his street address, to further authenticate the credential holder's identity. Some driver licenses list height and eye color, which can also be checked by the examiner.

+ **Reasonableness of Assertion.** Identity credentials that make an assertion about an individual's rights, position, or capabilities must also pass the "reasonableness test". For example, an examiner may reject or question a claim of assertion if the holder of the credential cannot reasonably make that assertion. If a man with long hair and a beard presents an active duty U.S. military ID card, an examiner may rightly question whether the holder of the credential can make that identity assertion. Someone who appears to be blind may hold a driver license, even though a blind person would not be licensed to drive. A police office who is conducting undercover operations may not appear to be a police officer, but he or she will have credentials that make that assertion, despite the officer's physical appearance.

+ **Electronic Verification.** If the credential supports it, a person's identity may be authenticated electronically. Some types of PKI certificates may be issued to a person only after a rigorous identity verification process. If the person who holds the credential is able to access the certificate's private key by using a password or PIN, and if there are other visual identification factors that can be verified, the person's identity may be considered to be properly authenticated.

7.4 Identity Proofing Processes

The identity proofing process involves verifying the identity of the Subject, based on information in identity documents provided by the Subject. Another part of the identity proofing process is collecting information on the Subject from source documents, correlating and comparing that information with corresponding information on other source documents, adjudicating and resolving differences among variations or inconsistencies in the information, and selecting the data that will appear on the new identity credential.

In most cases, the source documents are identity credentials themselves, so they are "breeder documents" for a new identity credential. Breeder documents may also be documents that are created and provided by the Subject, such as an application form. The information on such a document must be verified by the document examiner, because an application form usually becomes an information verification document. In most cases, an applicant must sign an application form, and thereby attests to the accuracy of the information the applicant has provided. If copies of the other identity documents are not retained by the issuing agency, the application form itself becomes the only breeder document the issuing authority can point to as the source of identity information.

The steps of the identity proofing process are:

+ Step 1 – The Subject presents source documents to an issuing authority or a representative of an issuing authority. In most cases, the issuing authority specifies the documents that are acceptable identity credentials, such as a driver license, passport, or bother certificate. The applicant may also be required to complete and sign an application form. The application form serves as a standardized data collection and presentation tool, but, as noted previously, the applicant's signature attests to his or her belief that the information on the form is accurate.

+ Step 2 – The credential examiner compares the information on the form with the corresponding information on the identity documents or credentials presented by the applicant. The examiner should compare the information on the application form (or the data received through another data collection process, such as completing an on-line application) with the corresponding data on the identity credentials.

  If there are inconsistencies in the data on the application and the credentials, the examiner must resolve the inconsistencies. Different addresses, many of which may no longer be valid, may appear on different documents. A woman's name on a birth certificate, for example, will not be the same as her married name. Long family names or names with complicated spellings may be shortened for certain types of identity documents. Major inconsistencies, such as differences in birthdates, Social Security numbers, or other data that should not change, must be resolved by the examiner.

> + Step 3 – Once the examiner has resolved any inconsistencies in the data on the documents or credentials, the examiner selects the identifiers that are to appear on the new identity credential. If there is inconsistent data on different identity credentials, the examiner must select which data element will be projected onto the new identity credential.

The new identity credential, which contains data that was derived from information on other identity credentials and documents, extends the chain of attestation of the validity of identifying information. In most cases, no link is maintained from an identity credential back to the breeder documents by which that information was obtained or validated. At best, the issuing authority may only retain the application form, with the signature that attests to the applicant's belief in the validity of the data. In many cases, privacy laws discourage credential issuing authorities from retaining copies of breeder documents. There are also cost and overhead considerations in maintaining documents and images in storage for long periods of time, and in providing systems to locate and retrieve those documents.

7.5   Biometrics and Identity Credentials

One of the most secure and more reliable ways to authenticate a person's identity is to verify that person's innate biological characteristics, which are referred to as *biometrics*. Each person's fingerprints, DNA, iris and retinal cell patterns, facial geometry, and heat signature are near unique to that person. These biometric measures, if properly recorded, validated, and embedded in identity credentials that are logically bound to a single person's identity, can provide the highest degree of identity authentication, short of personal recognition.

Some identity credentials already incorporate some types of biometrics, such as fingerprints. The Resident Alien Registration card, as well as several other immigration documents, have a fingerprint impression on the card. The identity verification and credential issuing process for the Department of Defense (DoD) Common Access Card (CAC) includes collecting fingerprints. For security reasons, the digital images of the CAC holder's fingerprints are not maintained on the CAC. Instead, the fingerprint images are stored on a DoD Enrollment Eligibility Reporting System (DEERS). A DoD building access or information system could access the fingerprint images to compare the digitized file to a fingerprint impression taken from someone seeking identity authentication.

Biometrics have unique characteristics over other forms of identity authentication, including:

> + **Unique Identifier.** A biometric identifier is usually unique to a single individual. Fingerprints are unique to a single individual, and are an unassailable identifier when a full set of prints, or prints from several fingers, can be used for identification. A person's DNA is not necessarily unique, but the chances of someone else who is not closely related having DNA identical to someone else's is extremely remote. Other, less widely used biometric identifiers, such as heat signatures, facial geometry, and iris and retinal patterns, are thought to be unique. However, heat signatures and facial geometry can be difficult to collect originally and sense reliably, and iris and retinal scans require special sensing equipment. If they are used at all, they are usually combined with other biometrics, to raise the level of assurance of positive identity authentication.

> + **Difficult to imitate or duplicate.** Fingerprints can be imitated and duplicated, and a fingerprint impression can be transferred or forged on an identification document. A false fingerprint can be created by taking an impression of a real fingerprint with wax, putty, or plastic, then using the negative of the print to mold a positive print. This can be used to print fingerprint impressions on false identity documents, or on a fingerprint reading device. However, it is not easy to use a false

fingerprint under the controlled circumstances of a building entry system or a system access control system. Furthermore, some new fingerprint scanners also test for a body heat signature on the finger, and a false or artificial fingerprint may not pass that test.

+ **Complexity.**One of the big advantages of biometric identifiers is that they can be complex, and therefore difficult to duplicate, or even to understand. Duplicating someone's DNA is beyond the capabilities of most identity credential counterfeiters, not to mention most biotechnologists, even those who have access to very sophisticated equipment. Their complexity decreases considerably the possibility that biometric identifiers can be forged, and that complexity raises the cost of counterfeiting biometric identifiers tremendously. Using several biometric identifiers is both costly and time-consuming, but they can identify an individual with greater levels of assurance than any other type of identifier.

7.5.1   "Something you have, something you know, something you are"

Both PKI and biometrics are more secure forms of identification verification because identification systems that use PKI and biometrics frequently rely on three-factor authentication. The three factors are frequently referred to as "*something you have, something you know, and something you are.*" That is, there are three factors that are used to positively identify the person. Taken together, they constitute a highly reliable identification verification. Two-factor authentication, which is a simpler, less secure form of authentication, uses only two authentication factors, such as a user name and password.

The PKI identity certificate on a DoD CAC is only issued to the CAC holder after a rigorous identity verification process. The purpose of the process is to determine with a high degree of assurance that the person applying for the certificate is indeed that person. The applicant must have a verifiable email address, and present two forms of identification credentials, one of which must be a government-issued photo identification, to two different credential examiners. The applicant must also agree to a background check, the objective of part of which is to verify the applicant's identity.

When the CAC is issued to the applicant, the identity certificate and its public and private keys are "burned" into the card's secure storage area. The applicant creates a six-digit PIN during the CAC issuance process, which the CAC holder uses to access the certificate's private key. The three authentication factors in CAC authentication are:

+ Something you have – The CAC card itself, which must be inserted in a smartcard reader to be "read" electronically

+ Something you know – The PIN, which allows the software on the PC or card reader device to access the certificate's private key

+ Something you are – The identity of the holder of the CAC, which is linked to the identity of the individual asserted on the identity PKI certificate

Two-factor authentication uses only two of the authentication factors. The user name or user ID is the equivalent of the "something you are", and the password is "something you know". Aside from not including a requirement to possess a tangible object, two-factor authentication lacks the same level of authentication as three-factor authentication. In most cases, a user ID is issued without much identity checking, or with only a cursory effort to verify the user's identification.

In many cases, a system administrator will issue a user ID, which acts as an account identifier, at the request of someone he or she knows is an authorized account requestor. The established procedure is usually that the system administrator relies on the authorized requestor's word that a user should be given a user ID. It is up to the requestor to establish who the user is, and whether he or she should be authorized access to the system.

In the PKI case, verifying the identity of a user and authorizing access to a system are two completely separate operations. Furthermore, the user's identity is clearly established and verified before the identity certificate is issued, and that identity is bound to the certificate when it is issued. Only the holder of that certificate is supposed to know the PIN to access the certificate's private key. So, when a user presents an identity certificate, the system has a high degree of assurance that the person who is using the identity certificate is indeed the person named in the certificate.

Granting access to a system or facility for that person is an access control decision. As is the case in a username/password environment, the system administrator must have the person named on the identity certificate on an access control list. Presenting an identity certificate is more secure than using a username and password. The PIN to access the private key of the certificate is not sent over the network, and it is not examined by the system. A password is usually sent to a system over the network for authentication, which presents its own set of security challenges.

7.6   Biometrics for Authentication vs. Forensics

Biometric identifiers can be combined with forensic identifiers to yield a more complete identity validation picture. Biometric identifiers are unique physical characteristics of an individual, such as fingerprints, retinal or iris patterns, palm prints, DNA, or other physical identifiers.

A forensic identifier identifies the manner in which an identifier is rendered, in order to assess its authenticity. For example, a person's written signature is widely used as a supplementary, but not a primary, means of identification, or of acknowledgement of a contract or transaction. Card-present credit card transactions are completed when the buyer signs the credit card receipt, or signs an electronic signature pad. There are variations in a person's signature from instance to instance, and it is not difficult to forge a signature that will pass as authentic.

However convincing a forged signature may appear, a forger cannot easily duplicate the way in which a person signs his or her name. That is, someone who signs his or her name uses variations in pen pressure, as well as changes in pen angle and pen velocity, that could be detected and recorded electronically. A record of these patterns would constitute forensic evidence of a person's signature – that is, the manner in which a person's signature is rendered. By combining the finished physical signature with the forensic record of how that signature was rendered, and examiner could make a more informed judgment of whether a signature is genuine.

Other types of forensic identifiers could be used to supplement biometric or physical identifiers. A fingerprint reader could sense the amount of pressure someone places on the fingerprint reader pad, or the heat signature of the person's finger. A voice analyzer could examine the intonation, inflection, pronunciation, accent, and speed of a person's speech, to develop a voiceprint of the patterns in a person's speaking voice.

This is not to say that forensic authentication is easy, or that the technology is ready to be widely deployed. The appearance of a person's signature may vary somewhat, depending on the circumstances under which the signature was rendered. Someone may sign a passport more clearly, and with more precision and deliberate effort, than he would sign a credit card receipt at a restaurant. Similarly, the forensic "signature" may vary depending on whether the person is standing or sitting down, the type of writing instrument, the type of writing surface, and other factors. Furthermore, the forensic evidence of a signature must be collected by an electronic sensing device. Consequently, its use would be limited to circumstances in which an electronic signature surface, such as a credit card purchase signature pad, could be used.

Forensic authentication only has limited applicability today, mostly as a means to supplement other physical and logical identifiers. Forensic authenticators are difficult to capture reliably and quickly. In most cases, the forensic system must take several samples of the same forensic evidence, in order to assess what it should expect in a typical forensic pattern, and what may be normal and acceptable variations from that pattern.

8.   Case Studies

As part of the study of identities and identity credentials, a number of widely-used identity credentials have been selected as case studies of identity credentials. There are, of course, a number of different types of identity credentials, but the few selected for closer study in this section are identity credentials that are both widely held and widely accepted for identity verification and validation purposes. One of them, the Social Security card, is not an identity document at all. However, it verifies that an individual - whose identity must be verified with other identity documents or credentials – has been assigned a valid Social Security number. A Social Security number is an essential "linking" identity, as it means that the individual is eligible to be legally employed, issued a driver license, open checking, savings, and other financial accounts, and file income tax returns.

In each case study, the identity credential will be examined to address four identity credential issues. These issues seek to identify for each credential the following characteristics:

+   Distinguishing goals of the credential

+   Data model of the credential

+   Physical structure

+   Physical and logical design limitations

8.1   U.S. Driver License

Even though the driver license has not been standardized from state to state, it has become the most widely available and most widely used identity document in the U.S.. The U.S. does not have a national ID card, so the driver license is often used as the *de facto* identity credential to fill this gap.

8.1.1   Distinguishing Goals

The driver license has a few, highly specific distinguishing goals, which include:

+   **Asserts the privilege to drive a motor vehicle.**The primary purpose of the driver license is to assert that the person identified on the document has met the qualifications of the state that issued the document to drive a motor vehicle. The license is typically restricted to certain categories of vehicles that the licensee is qualified to drive – automobiles, trucks, motorcycles, commercial vehicles (CDL), buses, and so forth.

+   **Verifiable identification of the licensee.**The license usually has enough information printed on it that an examiner can readily identify the holder. The photograph is the most commonly-used identifier, although until recently some states have not required photographs on all driver licenses, and many states still have driver licenses in circulation that do not have photographs. Driver licenses may have other biometric data on the holder that can be used for identification purposes. For example, a driver license may specify the holder's eye color, hair color, weight, and height, even though all but the holder's eye color may change during the validity period of the license. If the driver is involved in an accident or is stopped for a traffic violation, verifying the holder's identity is necessary for law enforcement purposes. If the holder is injured or killed in vehicle accident, this information is essential for notifying relatives and securing the victim's personal property.

+ **Official residence.** The driver license specifies the holder's home address, although it may, under some state laws, specify a business or other address. While this address is not necessarily binding for tax purposes, and it may change during the license's period of validity, it establishes that the holder was a resident of the state that issued the license, at least on the date that it was issued.

+ **Special requirements.** The driver license may also indicate special requirements that must be met in order to be allowed to drive. For example, the license may indicate that the driver must wear glasses, may only drive during daylight hours, or may only drive farm machinery on a farm or ranch. A learner's permit usually has similar restrictions on the number of passengers, hours of use, and relationships to passengers while driving. Because it is possible that the driver may be killed or severely injured while driving, the license is the logical place to put an indication that the holder is an organ donor, as well as any restrictions on the holder's organ donation wishes.

+ **Resistance to counterfeiting and tampering.** The acceptance of a driver license as a general-purpose identity document has created a thriving market for false, counterfeit, or altered driver licenses. Consequently, the driver license must be difficult to counterfeit or alter, yet relatively simple and economical to create. Many states use special plastic overlays or laminates, holographic icons, or embedded watermarks on driver licenses to make them difficult to counterfeit or alter without special equipment.

+ **Durability.** The validity period for a driver license is usually three to five years, so the physical credential media must be sufficiently durable to last at least that long. Data printed directly on the card's outer surface may wear off, so issuing agencies must develop license manufacturing technology that creates durable credentials, but that can be used in an office or driver license bureau environment.

8.1.2   Physical structure of credential

Most U.S. driver licenses are stiff plastic cards about the size of a credit card, with data printed on the surface of the card, or sealed beneath a specially laminated layer of plastic. The physical structure of the card has been designed to optimize durability and resistance to damage and tampering. Its size makes it easy to store and carry, and it can be copied easily on a flat-bed copier. Endorsements that specify extra driving privileges may be added to the basic license with adhesive stickers or other markings.

8.1.3   Design Limitations

Recent federal legislative changes, specifically the Real ID Act, will force state motor vehicle departments to standardize driver license content in the U.S.. While the result will not be the transformation of state driver licenses into a national identity card, standardizing state driver licenses will be beneficial to license holders as well as to law enforcement and homeland security personnel.

The Real ID Act, as well as changes in identity proofing and authentication by state motor vehicle departments, have improved the reliability of the driver license as an identity credential. One of the important characteristics of the driver license has been that it is both an identity credential and an assertion of the privilege to drive. In addition, the DL is almost always used as a source document for obtaining other credentials. The fraudulently issued DL will span other fraudulently issued credentials and invalid confirmation of identity assertions. In fact, the former has become a more important function of the credential than the latter. For residents who do not drive, most state motor vehicle departments offer an identity credential that is similar to, but visually distinguishable from, the state's driver license.

There are some limitations to the driver license credential, however, most of which are rooted in inconsistent application of standards by the more than 50 issuing authorities for driver licenses or non-driver identity cards. Some of these limitations are:

+ **Level of trust in issuing authority.** States and U.S. territories have reciprocity agreements among them that allow drivers from other states to be recognized as licensed drivers in other states. Driver licenses from other countries, however, may not be held in the same level of trust. Canada and the U.S. have an agreement that grants reciprocity for Canadian drivers in the U.S., and vice-versa. No corresponding agreement exists between the U.S. and Mexico, so a Mexican driver license may not be recognized in some U.S. states, and it may not be accepted in some places as an identity document.

+ **Electronic version of identity elements.** Many U.S. driver licenses have some or all driver license identity elements encoded electronically on the driver license. For example, the Virginia driver license has both one dimensional and two dimensional barcodes, which encode key data on the driver license holder, such as name, date of birth, and license expiration date. Other data that is not printed on the front of the license may also be encoded in the bar codes, such as weight and hair color. Some states encode key license holder data elements, such as name, date of birth, and license number, in a digital fingerprint that is encoded in the color photograph on the license. Many states do not use digital fingerprints, and different states' driver licenses encode more or fewer data elements than other states do. Presumably, conformance to the Real ID Act requirements will standardize what is encoded electronically on the license.

+ **Trail to source documents.** Few states maintain a traceable trail back to the breeder documents that were used to authenticate the subject's identity. Driver license issuing and identity proofing systems and requirements have changed substantially in the past few years, but a large percentage of driver licenses have been in effect for many years. In many cases, the breeder documents that were used to justify issuing the credential many years ago were never copied or recorded, so the trail to those documents has been lost.

8.1.4   Security Model

The security model of the U.S. driver license is changing because of the new role that has been thrust on this document – that of a general-purpose identity card. The *Real ID Act* will force more changes in the security model of the driver license, and make some aspects of the driver license security model relatively uniform across all U.S. driver licenses.

Compared to other documents, such as passports or resident alien registration card, most current U.S. driver licenses have a relatively simple security model. However, state motor vehicle departments have reacted to pressure from the Real ID Act, as well as acknowledging that more stringent identity verification methods are necessary, in order to improve the driver license security model.

The security model of the U.S. driver license can be evaluated against the following four criteria:

+ **Identity verification.** In most states, an applicant for a driver's license must present proof of both identity and of citizenship to obtain or renew a driver license. The Real ID mandate has strengthened states' efforts to validate the identity of driver license applicants. However, in most states, there is no requirement for a background or criminal check. Those steps would be expensive and time-consuming, and they are not part of the states' driver licensing requirements. Consequently, the strength of the identity verification process for a driver license depends on the authenticity of the identity and citizenship documents the applicant presents. However, given the widespread use of the driver license as the primary identification credential, it is possible that future threats may change requirements for verifying the identity of a driver license holder.

+ **Credential production.** Driver licenses have been counterfeited for many years, mostly to provide false identity documents for underage drinking. While underage drinking poses some public safety risks, it is not as serious a threat as terrorism. Most of the driver license document production improvements that have been made in recent years have been to prevent document counterfeiting for underage drinking purposes. However, those changes have also made it more difficult for terrorists to acquire false or counterfeit driver licenses, which they could use as identity documents to gain access to buildings or airplanes, or to buy weapons.

The security model for driver license production is directed at foiling attempts to counterfeit the driver license document, or to alter a genuine license. Many states issue driver licenses that are encased in special patterned laminates, or that employ foil optical variable devices (OVDs) that overlay the face and photograph of the driver license. These security features cannot be altered without damaging the credential, and they cannot be copied faithfully by standard scanners and digital copying devices. Some states use digital watermarks, which embed digital content in the background patterns on the license and in the holder's photograph. The digital watermark can be read by a special document scanner, which can determine if the information in the digital watermark matches the data printed on the license.

Some states supplement the security model by incorporating additional identifying information about the license holder in a magnetic strip or a barcode. However, this data can only be read with a compatible bar code reader or a magnetic stripe reader, which may not be generally available. As a result, supplementing the driver license data model with additional information is usually only as effective as the extent to which readers are available to capture and interpret that data.

State motor vehicle department employees who work at driver license issuing offices pose another threat to the driver license security model. They have access to the equipment, materials, and computer systems that are used to make bona fide driver licenses, and there have been cases of employees issuing driver licenses fraudulently. State motor vehicle departments must maintain strict controls over unauthorized access to driver license production systems, in order to maintain the integrity of the driver license security model. This includes controlling and monitoring access to driver license materials and production systems, auditing supply and production equipment usage, and establishing procedures that require the cooperation of several people to produce driver license credentials.

+ **Credential use.** Once it is in the license holder's possession, the issuing authority has no control over where or how that driver license is used. However, the Real ID Act requires states to make information about driver licenses available to other states' law enforcement and motor vehicle agencies. Sharing information about driver licenses improves the security model of the credential. It gives other states' law enforcement and motor vehicle agencies the ability to determine if the credential has been revoked, if the information printed on, such as the holder's birth date, matches the information that was verified when the credential was issued.

While law enforcement and motor vehicle agencies may be able to access driver license information, it may not be available to other agencies and organizations that accept the driver license as an identity document. Airport ticketing and security personnel do not check the validity of driver licenses, as they only verify that the passenger has an identity document that verifies the passenger's name. A passenger with a counterfeit driver license could attempt to fly under the name on the driver license. However, he may also need a credit card in the same name to pay for the flight and make the reservation, as paying in cash may alert security officials to potentially suspicious activity.

+ **Credential maintenance and termination.** Driver licenses may be revoked or suspended, usually for repeated traffic violations, driving under influence, or other driving infractions. The issuing state may suspend or revoke a credential, but it is only an administrative action until the driver license itself is seized or returned by the holder. Controlling possession of the credential is an issue in the security model of most physical credentials. However, if states' driver license databases are available to law enforcement officials in other states, and if those databases are checked in a traffic stop or other action, revoked or suspended driver licenses can be identified and seized.

Like other credentials that use photographs, the security model of the driver license does not accommodate maintaining a photograph that is any more current than the last one taken of the holder. Some states allow most drivers to renew a driver license by mail. In those cases, the new driver license uses the same photograph that was used previously. That photograph may be several years old, and may not reflect changes in the driver's appearance, such as amount, length, and color of hair. However, some identity documents, such as a U.S. passport, use photographs that can be ten years old by the time the passport expires, so this is not a serious flaw in the driver license security model.

If a driver renews an expired or about-to-expire driver license, or gets another license from another state, the issuing motor vehicle department usually seizes the old license before a new one is issued. This makes it difficult, but not impossible, for someone to hold driver licenses from more than one state. In addition, the new issuing state usually informs the old state that it has issued a new license, so that the old license can be revoked. This procedure is part of the driver license security model, although it is not clear if this is done uniformly or if procedures to do this are followed by every state.

8.2   U.S. Passport

The U.S. Passport is one of the most widely held identity credentials issued by the U.S. government. Its intent is to assert the U.S. citizenship of its holder, and to allow an examiner to verify the holder's identity, so that he or she may be extended the privileges and protection of a U.S. citizen while in other countries.

8.2.1   Distinguishing Goals

Key distinguishing goals of U.S. passports include:

+ **Essential travel document.** For most types of international travel, it is essential to possess a valid passport even before leaving most countries. Many countries in the European Union are an exception, as passport checks have been eliminated at many EU country borders. First, possession of a valid passport reduces significantly the chance that the traveler will be refused entry into the destination country, or into transit countries. Most important, the passport will be essential to be allowed to return to one's home country, or to the traveler's country of origin.

+ **Asserts U.S. citizenship** The identity verification and validation process used by the U.S. Department of State before issuing a passport is known to be fairly stringent, and the U.S. passport is familiar to law enforcement officials in most foreign countries. Consequently, the U.S. passport is an accepted identity credential almost anywhere overseas, whereas a state driver license would not be as widely accepted. Even though it may contain more identification data than a passport, a driver license carries no diplomatic obligation. A driver license is not issued by the U.S. government, so it does not imply citizenship. Therefore, a driver license does not carry any obligation for foreign countries to honor it as an identity credential.

+ **Amendment capability**Passport must have the capability to be amended, or to accommodate special markings, stamps, or documents, such as travel visas, entry permits, or entry and exit stamps. Many countries (including the U.S.) require citizens of most other countries to secure permission to enter the country, either with a visa or a travel permit. The visa or permit may be a separate travel document, or it may be affixed to or recorded in the traveler's passport. Most passports have blank pages, on which visas and travel permit stamps may be placed, so that they become a permanent part of the passport. To the extent that visas, entry and exit stamps, and other travel permission markings are added to the passport, the passport becomes a permanent record of the holder's overseas travel history.

8.2.2   Physical structure of credential

The U.S. Passport is a small, permanently-bound book with a flexible cover, about 3 ½" x 5"in size, containing 28 pages. Most of those pages are blank, and are intended to bear visas, entry permits, and other markings that indicate country entry and exit and immigration clearance stamps. The first page of the passport contains the holder's photograph, as well as the holder's name, and date and place of birth. The first page also asserts the holder's citizenship ("U.S.A"), as well as the date of issue and date of expiration of the passport.

Neither the passport holder's residence address nor his country of residence is permanently recorded in the passport. Those may change over the period of validity of the passport, without affecting the purpose or conditions of issue of the passport. Page 3 of the passport has blank lines where the holder may write a home address and the name and phone number of an emergency contact, but that information may change over the course of the standard 10-year validity period of the passport.

Travelers who expect that their passport pages will be filled may request a passport with 48 pages, or a special insert of more blank pages may be added to the standard passport.

Unlike driver licenses, U.S. passports are made in special passport processing offices, so the technology to create passports does not have to be suitable for use in an office environment. Passport photos are now scanned and printed directly on the first page of the passport, embossed with a special stamp, and sealed under a layer of patterned plastic laminate. These steps reduce the risk of tampering, and they make it difficult to create a counterfeit passport that cannot be detected by an experienced inspector.

In the future, the State Department plans to embed an contactless chip in the passport that can be read electronically. The chip will raise the security bar against passport counterfeiters, making it more difficult to create fake passports, or modify existing passports.

8.2.3   Design Limitations

The U.S. passport is an altogether sufficient document for the purpose for which it was intended, which is to assert citizenship for U.S. travelers while they are abroad. It is a durable document, it is fairly resistant to counterfeiting and tampering, and it has sufficient information to establish the holder's identity. It may be amended on its blank pages with visas and stamps to accommodate travel in counties that require additional travel permissions.

However, in its current form, the data in the passport is not easy to extract electronically. More stringent security and visa requirements for visitors to the U.S., as well as more intensive examination of citizens returning to the U.S. have placed a greater burden on U.S. immigration, customs, and transportation security agencies. However, there are two lines of forty four OCR characters on the data page of the passport can that can be read electronically.

However, an electronic element, such as a contactless chip planned for future versions of the passport, would allow additional information to be retrieved from the passport quickly. For example, a digitized file of the holder's photograph could be embedded in the chip, as well as fingerprints and other identity data that are not on the passport today. Additional security measures, such as encryption, would have to be added to protect the electronically-readable data.

8.2.4   Security Model

The security model of the U.S. passport can be evaluated against the same four security criteria as the driver license and other identity credentials in this section.

+ **Identity verification.**An applicant for a first-time or new passport must present evidence of both identity and citizenship. The applicant must present the two photographs and acceptable identity and citizenship documents to a passport application examiner, who verifies the authenticity of the documents, as well as the applicant's identity and citizenship. The examiner also verifies that the photographs are of acceptable quality, and that they are recent photographs of the applicant. As with the driver license, there is no background check or independent verification of the documents or the applicant. The examiner, who is frequently a U.S. Postal Service employee, serves as an agent of the Department of States to verify passport applicants' identities.

+ **Credential Production.**The security model for passport credential production is centralized in several U.S. passport production centers. Not only is it more efficient to operate a few high-volume passport production centers, but controlled, centralized operations have the potential to be much more secure operations as well. The photographs presented by the applicant are scanned, and a copy is printed on the data page of the passport. The printed image of the photo is embossed, and the image and the printed data on the page is sealed under a patterned laminate film. The paper stock and materials that are used in passport production are controlled, to prevent blank passport media from being used to create counterfeit credentials.

+ **Credential Use.**On international flights to destinations that require passports, airline personnel check the passports of departing passengers. The purpose of the passport check is to establish the identity of the traveler, but also to determine that each traveler will be qualified to enter the destination country. Passengers who arrive without a valid passport may be denied entry into the destination country, which may mean that the airline that brought the passenger may have to take him or her back. If the destination has an automated OCR character reading capability, each passport may be checked against an on-line database to identify fugitives or criminals.

+ **Credential maintenance and termination.**Standard U.S. passports are valid for ten years. Except for a few data changes, such as a change of name for marriage, there is little data on the passport itself that can change. In most cases, an expiring passport may be renewed, usually by mail, so there is no re-authentication of the subject in most passport renewals. An expired passport is not retained by the State Department. In fact, when a passport is renewed, the old passport is returned to the subject, who may use it as an identity document. To distinguish the passport as expired, the Passport Agency service center punches holes in the passport, to identify it as expired, or no longer valid for travel. Like driver licenses, passports may be revoked, suspended, or seized. Passports are the property of the U.S. State Department. Like most identity credentials, passports do not belong to the subject, but to the issuer.

8.3   Birth Certificate

The birth certificate was originally more of a ceremonial document that marked a life event, rather than an important identity document. However, birth certificates have changed considerably in the past few decades as the requirement to establish citizenship and age have become important components to qualify to obtain and hold other identity documents. In addition, birth certificates are an important data collection device, as they help establish birthrates, population growth or decrease, and health care facility requirements.

8.3.1   Distinguishing Goals

Key distinguishing goals of birth certificates include:

+   **Establish date and place of birth** The distinguishing goal of the birth certificate was originally to establish a person's date and place of birth. These facts were important to establish a person's eligibility or qualification for citizenship, as well as eligibility to attend school, join the military, get married, register to vote, hold a job, qualify for Social Security or a pension, and other purposes. Many birth certificates included the names of the mother and father of the child, as well as the attending physician, if there was one.

+   **Security, authentication.** Birth certificates have been issued by hospitals or by cities, counties, or states. Until recently, there were few standards that governed the format or content of the document. In many cases, the birth certificate was a certificate that was more suitable for *display* purposes than for use as an identity document. Increased emphasis security and authentication have increased the need for reliable and authentic documentation. To qualify for other identity documents, such as a driver license or a passport, an applicant must present a birth certificate as well as other documentation. Consequently, the traditional "presentation" birth certificate is no longer adequate to meet the new standards.

+   **Standards** In 2003, a panel sponsored by the U.S. Department of Health and Human Services (HHS) devised a recommendation for a standard U.S. birth certificate. The primary objective of the HHS standard birth certificate project was to improve and standardize the birth certificate as a tool for collecting vital statistics on child birth weight, ethnicity, maternal health, and a number of other factors. The proposed standard birth certificate would also serve as a much more reliable identity document. It requires far more information about the mother and father than most current birth certificates. That information would link the child and his or her parents more firmly to the information on the birth certificate, even as the child grew older into adulthood. For the report on the HHS project, see http://www.cdc.gov/nchs/data/dvs/panelreport_acc.pdf.

8.3.2   Physical structure of credential

The physical layout and content of a birth certificate varies considerably, as there are more than 6,000 authorities in the U.S. alone that issue birth certificates. The document may be an 8"x10" certificate, or a smaller document, although it is usually not small enough to fit into a wallet. The proposed HHS standardized birth certificate is a two-page form on 8 ½"x 11" paper.

Under normal circumstances, a birth certificate will be used as an identity document only a few times in a person's life, such as when registering to attend school, applying for a learner's permit or a first driver license, or applying for a first passport. Because it is used so infrequently, there is little need for the birth certificate to be in a smaller or more conveniently-stored size.

8.3.3   Design Limitations

The birth certificate is an unusual identity document, because it contains information that can be verified less reliably as time goes on. The identifying data is as old as the holder of the certificate, and another document, such as a driver license, may be required to link the birth certificate to the holder. The proposed HHS standard birth certificate contains significantly more information than traditional birth certificates, some of which may be verifiable over much of a person's lifetime.

If a birth certificate has been issued by a city or by most states, most of the information recorded on recent birth certificates is also maintained electronically. Cities' and states' obligations to report vital statistics to federal and state governments has driven the automation of many vital statistics systems, such as birth, death, and marriage certificates. This means that much of the information in recent birth certificates is maintained electronically, so that it can be reported to federal, state, and local authorities.

The proposed HHS standard for birth certificates represents a significant step in eliminating the inconsistency in U.S. birth certificates. Foreign birth certificates are another matter. Other countries may have completely different standards and procedures for recording and documenting births, as well as a number of different types of physical documents that are the equivalent of the birth certificate.

8.3.4   Security Model

Because of the wide variety of types and issuers of birth certificates, the security model of birth certificates is decidedly less rigorous than that of other identity documents.

+   **Identity Verification.** Paradoxically, identity verification for issuing a birth certificate is relatively strong, even though in use, the identity verification of the birth certificate is relatively weak. A birth certificate is usually issued within the first few days after a child is born, with identity information that is provided by one or both of the parents. It is one of the few identity documents that is issued with no input or acknowledgement from the subject. The identity verification part of the birth certificate security model is actually a process of establishing part of the subject's identity. Most hospitals will not release an infant unless the child has been named, although issuing the birth certificate document may occur somewhat later.

+   **Credential Production.** The security model for birth certificate production is weak, as there are a number of civil, medical, military, diplomatic, and religious organizations that have the authority to issue a birth certificate. In some religious denominations, an infant is not considered to have been officially named, nor is a birth certificate issued, until the child has been christened or undergone a religious ceremony. The U.S. Department of Health and Human Services has issued recommendations on a universal reporting system for vital statistics that serves as a standardized birth certificate form.

+   **Credential Use.** The security model of the use of the birth certificate depends on the existence of other identity credentials to corroborate the identity information claimed by the birth certificate. The credential use case security model for the birth certificate becomes weaker the older the subject is, as the subject's mother and father may die, or not be available or capable enough to confirm that the subject is the same individual listed on the birth certificate.

+   **Credential Maintenance and Termination.** The birth certificate is one of the only identity credentials that never expires, never needs maintenance, and is never terminated, revoked, or suspended. Particularly in the case of birth certificates issued by non-government agencies, the agency, organization, or institution may no longer exist, or it may not have records confirming issuing the birth certificate. Consequently, the security model for maintaining or terminating the birth certificate is strongest for permanent institutions, such as government agencies, but weakest for most non-government organizations.

8.4 Social Security Card

The Social Security card is such a simple document that it is surprising that it is considered an identity document at all. The card does not establish identity, and the first Social Security cards contained the phrase, "Not to be used for identification."

8.4.1 Distinguishing Goals

Key distinguishing goals of the social security card include:

+ **Name and SSN link** The Social Security card *only* links a name to a Social Security Number (SSN). However, the SSN is one of the most widely used identifying keys, linking the holder to a wide range of tax and financial records, driver license systems, travel documents, military records, and entitlement systems. The Civil Service Commission adopted the SSN as the official federal employee identifier in 1961, and the Internal Revenue Service adopted it as the official taxpayer ID number in 1962.

+ **Additional supporting evidence** Since 1978, the Social Security Administration has required all SSN applicants to provide evidence of age, citizenship, and identity. Aliens who are legally admitted to the U.S. are issued a Social Security number when they first enter the U.S.. Most infants born in the U.S. are issued Social Security numbers shortly after birth, as part of the documentation and recordkeeping process for obtaining a birth certificate.

+ **Objectives of the card** The initial objective of the Social Security card was to give the holder a tangible record of his or her SSN, so that the Treasury Department could credit payroll deductions to the correct Social Security account. The original Social Security cards also listed the date the number was issued, and provided a place for the holder to sign the card. When the first Social Security cards were issued in 1936, the new Social Security Administration did not have any field offices, so the cards were issued by "typing centers" at more than 1,000 U.S. Post Offices.

+ **Types of cards** Today, the Social Security Administration issues three types of Social Security cards. The first is the standard Social Security card, which is issued to U.S. citizens, and to aliens who are legally allowed to live and work in the U.S. The second, which is issued to people who have been admitted to the U.S., but who do not have Department of Homeland Security (DHS) permission to work in the U.S., bears the legend, "Not Valid for Employment". The third type, issued to aliens who have been legally admitted to the U.S. and who have permission to work temporarily in the U.S., bears the legend, "Valid for Work Only with DHS Authorization." The Social Security Administration and DHS operate an automated system to help employers match a SSN with the holder's name and data of birth.

8.4.2 Physical structure of credential

The Social Security card is a valuable document, because it is required to establish the right to work in the U.S., but it has relatively few physical security features. It is a simple paper card, printed on high-quality paper, and it is about the size of a credit card. As valuable as it is, it incorporates few sophisticated anti-counterfeiting characteristics, and its only immediately verifiable identity elements are the holder's name and signature.

Counterfeiters have long mastered the art of creating false or altered Social Security cards. The SSA has taken steps to make the card more difficult to counterfeit, such as using high-quality paper, special security devices, and special printing techniques. In order to protect the card, some people laminate the card in plastic. However, the Social Security Administration considers lamination to be an improper alteration of the card, as it makes it difficult to evaluate the quality and feel of the paper, or identify a counterfeit or altered card. Some companies will make a more durable metal or plastic facsimile of a Social Security card. The Social Security Administration does not consider metal or plastic replicas of cards to be valid substitutes for real cards either.

8.4.3   General Observations

The Social Security card is probably the least secure of an individual's important identity documents, but the expense of making it more secure may not be worthwhile. What is most important about the Social Security card is the Social Security number, and its linkage to the holder's name and data of birth. An individual's Social Security number is so widely used as a key for tax, financial, entitlement, and other records that a false Social Security number may have only limited utility. On the other hand, obtaining another person's Social Security number is key to identity theft, though it is more likely that an identity thief will get the number from a paycheck stub, tax return, or some other document, instead of a Social Security card.

The danger is that a false Social Security number, a counterfeit Social Security card, or a fraudulently-obtained Social Security number can be used to obtain other identity documents, or to get a job. However, long-term use of a false number or another person's Social Security number is difficult to sustain. Except for cases of identity theft, using a false Social Security number initiates a web of identity documents, financial and payroll accounts, and other permanent records that will not match to a real person.

Legislation has been introduced in Congress several times in recent years to make the Social Security card a more useful and verifiable identity document. Some of these bills have proposed that the holder's photograph and other security features be included on new versions of the card.

However, most of the proposed changes would make the Social Security card similar to a driver license. Most of these proposals have not been widely supported because of the cost of the proposed changes, and because a valid driver license can be linked to the holder's SSN. In fact, being able to cross-validate the Social Security number with the identity of the person who holds a driver license is an important identity validation step.

8.4.4   Security Model

+   **Identity Verification.** The Social Security card security model requires that an applicant be able to prove only his identity, even though the Social Security card is also required for the subject to be legally employed. That is, a subject may obtain a Social Security card because it is a required document for employment, but the subject may not necessarily be eligible to be employed legally. In that sense, the security model of the Social Security card only links the Social Security number to the subject's name, not to any specific use of the credential.

+   **Credential Production.** The Social Security card is a simple document that contains nothing more than the subject's name and Social Security number. Like many other identity documents, the credential production security model relies on high-quality, controlled production media and materials, in order to make it difficult to produce false Social Security cards, or alter real ones. However, since the Social Security card has no other identifying information than the subject's name, there are few security devices on the card itself.

+   **Credential Use.** The Social Security card is not a general-purpose identity document, such as a driver license, so the security model for its use as an identity credential is limited. Like a subject's birth certificate, the Social Security card is usually used with another identity credential, such as a driver license, that provides more current and more verifiable identity information,

+ **Credential Maintenance and Termination.** Except for special circumstances, such as some cases of identity theft, a Social Security number is issued for life. Consequently, the security model of the Social Security card and, more important, the Social Security number, has few implications for the maintenance of the credential. In fact, the credential itself is not as important as the number and its link to an individual's name. When a subject dies, however, and the Social Security Administration learns about it, the Social Security number is marked as inactive. This does not terminate the Social Security number, however, as it may be used for years after the subject's death to pay income and estate taxes, to determine survivors' financial benefit eligibility, to identify the subject's remaining financial accounts, and to settle the subject's estate.

8.5   PIV Card

The objective of the federal PIV program is to provide secure, authenticated identity credentials to all employees and officials of the federal government. The PIV card, which builds on the experience of the NIST smart card research and development efforts, which included input from DoD on their experience with the CAC. The DoD CAC, is intended to serve as an employee identity badge and a building and facility access pass. It will also allow the user to login to government computer networks, and access government IT systems.

8.5.1   Distinguishing Goals

Key distinguishing goals of the PIV card include:

+ **HSPD-12 and FIPS 201.** Homeland Security Presidential Directive Number 12 (HSPD-12) requires a secure identification credential for all federal employees and contractors. Federal Information Processing Standard (FIPS) 201 describes the architecture and technical requirements for the PIV identification credential card that satisfies the HSPD-12 requirements. The FIPS 201 standard describes requirements for personal identity proofing, registration, and issuing PIV cards. In order to support technical interoperability among PIV systems of Federal departments and agencies, the standard also describes the card elements, system interfaces, and security controls required to securely store, process, and retrieve identity credentials from the card. The physical characteristics of the card, its storage media, and the data elements that make up identity credentials are specified in this standard.

+ **SP 800-73.** The interfaces and card architecture for storing and retrieving identity credentials from a smart card are specified in Special Publication 800-73, Interfaces for Personal Identity Verification. Similarly, the interfaces and data formats of biometric information are specified in Special Publication 800-76, Biometric Data Specification for Personal Identity Verification. [SP8000-73]

+ **PIV and DoD CAC** The PIV card is similar to the DoD CAC, but there are differences between them. For example, CAC PKI certificates use a ten digit number, which is appended to the card holder's name, in the Subject Alternate Name field. The number is generated by a DoD personnel system, which also stores the images of the two fingerprints that were scanned when the CAC holder received the CAC. DoD systems may use that number to identify the user. The PIV card has a similar identifying number, the Federal Agency Smart Credential Number (FASC-N) in the Card Holder Unique ID (CHUID), The FASC-N is not the same thing as the DoD number on the CAC certificates.

8.5.2   Physical Structure of Credential

The FIPS 201 standard requires that PIV cards contain a photograph, as well as certain mandated and optional printed information and mandated and optional machine-readable data. The mandated data includes the photograph, the holder's name and affiliation (e.g. Employee, Contractor, etc.), the agency or organization, and the card expiration date. The card may also have a seal of insignia identifying the issuing agency, an optional space for the card holder's signature, and other optional data elements.

The optional card elements include a signature block, colored or patterned borders, bands, or outlines that indicate regular employees, contractors, or foreign nationals, military or civilian rank or grade, a 2D barcode or magnetic strip, physical characteristics of the card holder (eye and hair color, height), and an indicator that the holder is an Emergency Responder Official.

The PIV also contains logical data elements that can be used to verify the cardholder's identity at graduated assurance levels. The mandatory logical data elements are a PIN, the CHUID, a digital certificate, and two fingerprint images. Other optional logical data elements, such as additional digital certificates, may be added to the card.

At the time the card is issued, a full set of fingerprints is taken, but digital images of only two fingerprints are stored on the card. In addition to the photograph on the face of the card, a digital version of the photograph image may also be stored on the card. The reason for storing digital versions of the cardholder's picture and fingerprints and on the card is to allow more convenient use of those images for physical and logical access. For example, a cardholder could be required to swipe his card at a building entry point, which would read the digital facial image and fingerprint files. A building security guard could display the cardholder's picture on a monitor, instead of having to examine the card, and a fingerprint reader at the entrance point could confirm that the person is the cardholder.

8.5.3   General Observations

The PIV card provides federal government agencies the same kind of high quality, high assurance identity credential that DoD military personnel, civilian employees, and contractors already have. If it is used properly, the PIV card can increase security for federal facilities and information systems.

Federal agencies may benefit from studying the DoD experience with the CAC, in order to attempt to avoid the problems that the DoD has encountered in utilizing the CAC. The DoD CAC is the world's largest implementation of PKI-enabled smartcard identity credentials, and the PIV program is even larger. Some of the lessons that have been learned in the DoD CAC program that are applicable to the PIV program are:

+ **Underestimating the challenge or the opportunity.** Each federal agency is responsible for running its own PIV card program, which will be both a challenge and an opportunity. There is no central federal agency that will run the PIV program, although the General Services Administration has issued procurement specifications for PIV cards, and NIST is running tests to establish interoperability standards. The PIV specifications in FIPS 201 and NIST SP 800-73 give each agency some latitude in the content and data element layout of the card, so they can customize it for their own purposes. Asides from the interoperability challenge, the PIV program is also an opportunity for federal agencies to develop a standardized identity credential that can be used throughout federal agencies.

+ **Under-or unfunded mandates.** The PIV program was initiated by the HSPD-12 Presidential Directive, which did not provide any agency with funding for the PIV program. Federal agencies are expected to fund the program from their current budgets. While federal agencies recognize the need and the requirement to meet the PIV requirements, it is up to each agency to fund the program as it sees fit. This may mean that some agencies will do a better job than others in launching, securing, managing, and maintaining the program.

+ **PIN reset.** The PIV card has a numeric PIN associated with the card's digital certificates. The subject will select the PIN, and use the PIN to access the private keys of the certificates on the card to identify himself or herself, or to apply a digital signature to a document or message. As a security measure, the DoD CAC allows the user to try to enter the correct PIN three times. After the third consecutive incorrect PIN try, the CAC will not accept any more PIN attempts. The PIV card, which is similar to the CAC, may have a similar security feature for which CPR or equivalent facilities will have to be provided.

+ **Building access infrastructure.** One of the requirements of the PIV program is that the PIV card be used for building access. Building access systems, if they exist, will have to be upgraded and standardized to use the PIV card, as well as the PIV cards held by employees and contractors of other federal agencies. The PIV standard also allows for the use of contactless PIV cards that can be read by a proximity card reader. The contactless card interface standard also permits a contactless card reader to pull the digital image of the PIV cardholder from the card, so that it can be displayed for a building entrance guard. If this capability is used, systems will have to be installed that can read contactless cards reliably, and display digital images.

+ **Network smartcard login issues.** The PIV card is to be used for accessing both federal facilities and federal information systems. While it is not addressed specifically, this may mean that the PIV card must be used to logon to a computer network, such as an Windows network in a federal agency's offices. Implementing and supporting smartcard login is not a trivial exercise, particularly if there are several different types of networks in use besides Windows. Current version of Windows have native support for PKI certificates and smartcard login, but older versions of Windows do not. In addition, to use the PIV card for network login, each workstation must have a smartcard reader and smartcard middleware that allows it to read the smartcard and extract the certificates. Unless smartcards are in use already, few federal agencies have smartcard readers and middleware installed. Using the PIV card for network login would require a substantial investment in hardware, software, and support, the cost of which would have to be borne by the agency as part of the unfunded mandate.

+ **PKI enabling systems and applications.** The PIV card contains PKI certificates, but most federal agency applications and systems have not yet been modified or created to understand how to use PKI certificates. PKI-enabling applications and systems has been a DoD requirement for several years, but few systems and applications have been PKI-enabled. Federal agencies will have the same problems, particularly with legacy and mainframe applications.

+ **CRLs and validating certificates.** The digital certificates on the PIV card will have expiration dates, after which time they will no longer be valid. If a digital certificate is revoked because the subject retired or is no longer employed by the federal government, the certificates must be registered on a *Certificate Registration List* (CRL). The CRL must be distributed or made available to any federal agency that accepts PIV certificates, to determine if a certificate is still valid. Maintaining, distributing, and using CRLs to authenticate identity credentials is another one of the challenges that federal agencies must meet.

8.5.4   Security Model

+ **Identity Verification.** An applicant for a PIV card will be subjected to the same type of identity verification process as is used for the DoD CAC. That is, the applicant must complete an application form and present identity documents, such as a driver license or a passport, that are reviewed by someone who is the equivalent of a PIV trusted agent. The application initiates a background check of the subject, which servers as a secondary confirmation of the subject's identity. With these identity verification checks in place, the security model for PIV identity verification is relatively strong.

+ **Credential Production.** The PIV card will be similar to the DoD CAC, which is produced in decentralized RAPIDS workstations. The credential production security model of the CAC does not require a highly controlled production facility, only a highly controlled credential creation workstation and an operator who controls access to credential media. Federal agencies are free to devise their own security model for PIV credential production. Even if several federal agencies consolidate and share credential production facilities, or contract out credential production responsibilities to third parties, they would still have to devise a credential production security model that could meet the challenges of counterfeit credentials, theft or misuse of credential media, and security of the credential production devices.

+ **Credential Use.** The PIV card incorporates digital certificates, one of which will be an identity certificate. If systems are enabled to use the PIV digital certificates, and network logon is enabled for federal agencies' networks, the credential use security model will be relatively strong. The alternative to using digital certificates is username and password, which is a much less secure access control measure.

+ **Credential Maintenance and Termination.** The security model for PIV credential maintenance and termination is similar to that of the DoD CAC. Issuing agencies will have to maintain and distribute CRLs of revoked or suspended certificates, and they will have to develop policies and procedures to issue new certificates and PIV credentials when subjects change jobs, agencies, or possibly security clearance levels. Federal agencies will also have to develop policies and procedures for collecting, controlling, and destroying credentials that are no longer valid, or that belong to subjects who are no longer authorized to hold them.

8.6   e-Credentials

<This section is planned to contain a case study of a purely electronic identity credential, i.e., a credential without specific physical form, just an information structure. The Finnish EID could be used as the case study, or a Federal certificate.>

An e-Credential is an identity credential that is purely an electronic credential, and is not necessarily tied to a specific physical credential token. The e-Credential establishes identity, and it may be used to authenticate the Subject, or to sign documents and messages, or to encrypt data. A PKI certificate is an e-Credential, but the key consideration is that as an E-Credential, the PKI certificate could be used on its own, instead of being tied to a specific physical identity token.

For example, a PKI certificate e-Credential could be housed on a smartcard. In most cases, it might be most convenient if it were, because the card itself could serve as an identity document or a building pass. However, the e-Credential could be housed on a USB token, a floppy disk, or on a computer, cell phone, or other mobile device. In those cases, the e-Credential would exist only in electronic form.

The distinction between a PKI certificate on a smartcard, such as a PIV card, and a PKI certificate that is not on a similar identity toke, may seem to be semantic rather than real. However, some government agencies have proposed introducing an e-Credential, and it is worth examining the implications of e-Credentials, and their limitations. The federal government's X.509v3 PKI certificate is potentially an e-Credential, and the Finnish government allows the use of electronic identity credentials on identity cards, as well as on other electronic devices.

8.6.1   Finnish Citizen Certificates

The Finnish government is issuing all Finnish citizens identity cards that contain PKI certificates. The certificates act as electronic identification (EID) credentials.

The electronic identity card is a secure network key for all on-line services which require personal identification, such as all government and many private sector services. The card enables the service provider to reliably identify the user. The card is also an official travel document for Finnish citizens in Northern Europe as well as in European Union countries.

The primary certificate on the Finnish citizen identity credential is the Citizen Certificate. This certificate contains standardized personal data, such as a citizen's first name, family name, and an electronic client identifier. The Citizen Certificate is a network key for e-services requiring strong identification. Two codes are needed to use online services with the Citizen Certificate. The first is an identification code (PIN1) to register for online services. A signature code (PIN2) is used to sign documents electronically.

The Citizen Certificate is an example of an e-Credential because it is not necessarily housed only on a Finnish identity card. The certificate may be on a bank card, such as a credit card or an ATM card. A bank in Finland puts a Citizen Certificate on its bank cards, so that the holder of the card can be used for banking services, in addition to the same online services as a regular ID card.

A mobile version of the Citizen Certificate can be attached to the SIM card of a mobile device, such as a cell phone. With the mobile certificate, a Subject can identify himself or herself to various public- and private-sector services through a computer or a mobile device. Cellular phone companies and their phones must support mobile Citizen Certificates, and to date, only two Finnish cell phone companies support the use of mobile certificates. Finland has one of the highest rates of mobile phone usage, so mobile certificates are likely to be supported by more of the country's cellular carriers.

8.6.2   e-Credentials and Container Independence

In theory, the physical independence of e-Credentials from underlying identity tokens gives them great flexibility. However, that independence may also be a liability, and in practice, measures to secure e-Credentials may mitigate their flexibility.

The most evident downside of e-Credentials is that they cannot be read without specialized electronic equipment, such as a card or certificate reader, a computer, or a specialized display device. If the e-Credential is housed on an identity card, an inspector may read the data printed on the identity card or document, and see the photograph, signature, or other physical identifying information. An e-Credential alone has no physical embodiment, so its data can only be read electronically.

The more problematic aspect of the e-Credential is that it cannot be completely independent of any other system if it has a component or data that is either secret or encrypted. If there is encrypted or secret data, there must be a way to decrypt it, such as with a private key. For security reasons, the private key can't be on the electronic credential itself, but it must be held somewhere else. The "somewhere else" component means that the e-Credential is no longer an independent data object, in that its operation must rely on some other entity or storage container that holds the private key.

9.   Miscellaneous Topics

This section highlights some current "trends and innovations" in the Identity area and will be expanded as needed.

9.1   Identity Firewalls – a possible solution to Identity theft

The practice of using unrelated information to identify individuals in business transactions is a prime factor in making identity-theft easy. In the U.S.A this is usually the use of social security number and/or driver's license number. This can be reversed by each industry creating and adopting identification and authentication procedures that result in unique industry-specific identities for their customers. By creating these "identity firewalls", and using significantly stronger technology – Digital Certificates and multi-factor authentication tokens – to manage the credentials, consumers, businesses and government can minimize the risk and costs of identity-theft.

An efficient compromise would be to have customer identification be consolidated around "industries'. For instance, everyone will, typically, deal with one or more of the following seven "industries" in their lifetimes:

    i.   The Government – Federal, State and Local agencies

    ii.   Healthcare – Hospitals, Pharmacies, Insurance companies, HMO's, etc.

    iii.   Education – Schools, Colleges, Universities, Professional associations, etc.

    iv.   Financial – Banks, Brokerages, Thrifts, S&L's, Insurance companies, etc.

    v.   Retailers and E-commerce sites – Stores, Airlines, Hotels, Car Rental, etc.

    vi.   Other Services – Legal, Accounting, Gaming, etc.

    vii. An   Employer

Building on the premise of using Digital Certificates and multi-factor authentication tokens to identify and authenticate individuals, each of the above industries could establish a single authority to identify and then, issue authentication tokens and Digital Certificates to customers, based on a rigorous and independent process that would apply to all businesses within that industry. Existing not-for-profit industry associations could assume this function for the benefit of their members to get the process jump-started. [STRAUTH]

9.2   Challenges in Identity Management

Managing the full range of identity events, information, and documents, from identity verification to issuing identity documents and credentials to authenticating identities at point of use, presents a set of challenges in itself. Identity management processes frequently present other, unique challenges that must also be resolved for identity systems to be practical. Many of these challenges are not evident until they are encountered. Resolving many of them may take an inordinate amount of time and energy, regardless how simple they may seem. Some of these challenges are:

9.2.1   Reconciling and merging identity sets

It is common for organizations have a number of systems and databases that hold identity information on the organization's employees, users, or subscribers. The organization may want to merge disparate data sets, or map a master list against entries in other identity databases. The objective is develop a master identity list, in order to integrate identity databases,

This reasonable objective may be more difficult to achieve than it would seem. Each database may not list everyone in the organization, and the identifying information in each database may be slightly different for the same individual. The challenge, which seems simple in theory, but which is difficult in practice, is to match the information in separate databases to the same person.

For example, an organization's HR department may maintain a number of databases for employee payroll, benefits, and evaluation. The organization's security department may maintain another database for employee ID cards, building access, and security clearances. The IT department may maintain another set of databases for network logon, system access, and account access controls.

Even if the organization uses a unique identifier, such as an employee number or a Social Security number as a common identifier key, it may find that there are significant discrepancies between the identifying information for the same person in each of these databases. These discrepancies can make what may seem to be the simple task of merging or cross-referencing individual identity information a significantly more difficult task. A large percentage of the identity information may be resolved to a specific individual. However, a number of identity records will most likely not map accurately, or not map to any other record at all. It is this group which can only be resolved by labor-intensive, manual cross-checking of identity information.

For example, an HR database may list a person's full name (first, middle and last), Social Security number, employee ID number, date of birth, home address, employment date, pay grade, and other personal information. A network logon database may have the same person registered by last name and first name only, or by a truncated, eight-character combination of the person's first initial and the first seven characters of his or her last name.

Without any other corresponding information in either database, an automated database mapping system may be designed to make a reasonable guess that the two records refer to the same person. However, people would have to review the results manually to determine if the conclusion the computer program drew were correct.

The matter may be made more difficult by restrictions on data access, either for security, privacy, legal, procedural, or other reasons. That is, the people who have the task of resolving the cases that cannot be resolved by automated mapping or matching systems may not be permitted to access all parts of the records in question.

9.2.2   Multiple ID credentials

Many identity credential systems have been designed according to the "one person, one credential" principle. Ideally, a subject should only have a single identity credential issued by a specific system. A person should only have one driver license, issued by a single state. While it is possible that a person may have a driver's license from more than one state, an individual should not have two drivers' licenses from the same state.

Some identity credential systems do allow a single subject to have more than one identity credential issued by the same system. However, multiple credentials issued by the same credentialing authority are redundant at best, and potentially dangerous at worst.

For example, a DoD contractor who is also a military reservist may have two or more DoD CACs. The CACs belong to the same person, but the email address on each CAC's PKI certificates will most likely be different.

9.2.3   Role-based ID credentials

Role-based identity credentials identify the role that a person is performing, not necessarily the person who is performing the role. For example, a watch officer on a ship may, during the time he or she is on watch, use a role-based credential for the use of the watch officer. To indicate that the watch duties have been performed, or that they have been performed properly.

Role-based credential systems assume that the people who use them are authorized to do so. The watch officer, for example, may be on an access control list to use the credential. The credential access systems may be designed so that the watch officer must use a personal identity credential, such as a CAC, to gain access to the role-based credential.

9.2.4   Auditing identity credential use and validity

It is one thing for a credentialing authority to issue credentials, and another for that authority to determine which of those credentials are valid and in use, and if the subjects to which they were issued are still authorized to have them. Credentialing authorities should conduct periodic audits of their credential records to weed out expired or invalid credentials. Ideally, the system that maintains credential records should have an automatic update feature, to pull records of credentials after their expiration date, or to flag them to determine if they have been renewed.

Credentialing authorities for closed, controlled groups of credential holders should also map their issued credential database periodically against a database of authorized credential holders. For example, a company that issues identity credentials to its employees should map its records of employees who have credentials against the company's current employee files, and reconcile any discrepancies between the two.

9.2.5   Foreign identity credentials

English is the language most commonly used in identity documents that are intended to be used in other countries, such as passports, visas, and other travel documents. However, many identity documents that were not intended to be used outside of their country of origin may not be in English, or have data fields that are identified in English. The data fields on a Chinese driver license, for example, may be written in Mandarin Chinese, and not in English.

Of course, a Chinese traveler would use a passport, not a Chinese driver license, as a travel document. However, if that person applied for identity documents in the U.S., he might use the driver license, as well as his passport, as forms of identification.

The foreign identity credential problem does become a problem in countries that have heavy immigration flows, especially from non-English-speaking counties. Some identity document, such as birth certificates, may be written only in the subject's native language, or in a dialect of that language.

9.2.6   Practical biometrics

Biometric identifiers, such as fingerprints, retinal scans, and DNA samples, have been proven to be reliable identifiers. They are potentially more reliable than most identity documents alone, even ones with photographs, because biometrics are difficult to fake or forge. Further, the technology for counterfeiting biometrics is not widely available, if it even exists at all.

As attractive as biometric identifiers may be, making them simple, reliable, and fast is a problem that grows with the number and type of biometrics used. For example, some identity credential systems incorporate physical fingerprint images on the credential, or store digital fingerprint images on or off the credential. However, taking an inked fingerprint from a subject, reading that print, and establishing that it is a match, are tasks that should be performed by a trained technician.

Electronic fingerprint images do not necessarily solve this problem. The capabilities and sensitivities of electronic fingerprint sensors vary, and the image taken at a building entry point or an ID verification station may be of greater or lesser quality than the original reference image. Fingerprint scanner vendors may use different algorithms and techniques to analyze a fingerprint image, which may lead to inconsistent results.

The problem of quickly and reliably matching fingerprints or other biometrics becomes much more difficult as the number of people in the identity pool increases. Some laptop computers and cell phones have fingerprint sensors, so that only the owner of the device can use it. These sensors are relatively simple devices, and they only need to match a fingerprint image against a single reference image.

Finding a match to a fingerprint image against thousands or millions of fingerprint images is a much more difficult problem. In practice, fingerprint images are used as secondary identifiers, after a photograph or other data has been analyzed. Furthermore, the fingerprint or fingerprint image need only match the image or images stored on the identity document or in offline storage.

APPENDIX A: Acronyms

The definitions provided below are defined as used in this document. The same terms may be defined differently in other documents.

AAMVA	American Association of Motor Vehicle Administrators
CAC	Common Access Card
CHUID	Card Holder Unique ID
DEERS	DoD Enrollment Eligibility Reporting System
DHS	Department of Homeland Security
DL/ID	Driver's License and Personal Identification
DNA Deoxyribo	Nucleic Acid
DoD	Department of Defense
FIM	Federated Identity Management
FIPS	Federal Information Processing Standard.
FISMA	Federal Information Security Management Act
HR Human	Resources
HSPD	Homeland Security Presidential Directive
IAB	Internet Architecture Board
IANA	Internet Assigned Numbers Authority
ICAO International	Civil Aviation Organization
INS	Immigration and Naturalization Service
ID Identity	
IESG	Internet Engineering Steering Group
IETF	Internet Engineering Task Force
ISO International	Standards Organization
ISOC Internet	Society
IT Information	Technology
MRTD	Machine Readable Travel Documents
NCHS	National Center for Health Statistics
NIST	National Institute of Standards and Technology
NTWG	New Technologies Working Group
OASIS	Organization for the Advancement of Structured Information Standards
OTP One-Time	Password
OATH Open	Authentication
OCR	Optical Character Recognition
OMB	Office of Management and Budget
PDI	Personal Data Interchange
PIM Personal	Information Manager
PIN Personal	Identification Number
PIV Personal	Identity Verification
PKI	Public Key Infrastructure
SAML	Security Assertion Markup Language
SGML	Standard Generalized Markup Language
SSN	Social Security Number
UDDI	Universal Description, Discovery and Integration

URL   Universal Resource Locator
U.S. United   States
USB   Universal Serial Bus
UTC   Universal Time Coordinated [global standard]
XML Extensible   Markup Language

APPENDIX B: References

[GRUBER]   T. R. Gruber. Toward principles for the design of ontologies used for knowledge sharing. Presented at the Padua workshop on Formal Ontology, March 1993.

[FIPS201]   Federal Information Processing Standard 201-1, Personal Identity Verification (PIV) of Federal Employees and Contractors, June 2006.

[SP800-73]   Special Publication 800-73-1, Interfaces for Personal Identity Verification, (March 2006).

[STRAUTH]   www.strongauth.com

APPENDIX C: Glossary

Applicant - A person who has applied to become a key holder, prior to the time at which keys and certificates are issued to and accepted by them.

Authentication - The process of identifying an individual, in computer systems this is usually based on a username and password. In security systems, *authentication* is distinct from *authorization*, which is the process of giving individuals *access* to system objects based on their identity. Authentication merely ensures that the individual is who he or she claims to be, but says nothing about the access rights of the individual.

Authenticator – Secrets that create the binding between credentials and it's presenter.

Authorization – Permission to perform some action.

Credentials – Certificate or document attesting to the truth of certain stated facts.

Enrollment Service - The entity that manages the process of a certificate applicant applying for a certificate.

Identity Credential – Information (electronic or printed) that seeks to either uniquely identify or provides qualifications or defining attributes about an individual identity.

Identification – In a biometric security system, the process of comparing a biometric data sample against all of the system's database reference templates in order to establish the identity of the person trying to gain access to the system.

Investigation Service – An entity that examines credentials and evaluates their authenticity.

Issuing Authority – An entity that issues credentials, and that updates credential status after issuance.

Judicial Authority – An entity that performs dispute resolution; it may be a legal authority, or an arbitrator whose actions are agreed to by both parties involved in the dispute.

References – Documents or information used to verify a Subject's identity before issuing a credential.

Registration Authority - An entity that registers applicants for keys and certificates, verifies user requests for a digital certificate, and tells the certificate authority it may issue a certificate.

Relying Party - A recipient who acts in reliance on a certificate and digital signature.

Sponsor – An entity that is authorized to make a request that a certificate be issued to a subject or entity, and that attests that the subject has the need and the right to hold a certificate.

Subject - A field in a certificate that identifies the person or entity to whom the certificate is issued; also, an authorized entity that uses a certificate as applicant, subscriber, recipient or relying party, but not including the CA issuing the certificate.

Transaction Intermediary – An entity that is involved in or handles a credential transaction, but that does not act as the ultimate arbiter of the transaction's authenticity or trustworthiness.

Trust – Permitted action to be performed only for the intended purpose.

Validation Service - An entity that receives requests from Relying Parties to determine the status of a credential, and that returns the status of the credential, as updated by the Issuing Authority.

Validation – Verification that something is correct or conforms to a certain standard. In data collection or data entry, it is the process of ensuring that the data that are entered fall within the accepted boundaries of the application collecting the data. For example, if a program is collecting last names to be entered in a database, the program validates that only letters are entered and not numbers; or in a survey collecting data in the form of "yes" or "no" questions, the program validates that only those responses are used and not some other word.

Verification – In a biometric security system, the process of comparing a biometric sample against a single reference template of a specific user in order to confirm the identity of the person trying to gain access to a system.